Little House of Quilts

of

14 Nostalgic Quilts *and* Projects Inspired
by the Writings of *Laura Ingalls Wilder*

LAURA STONE ROBERTS

CINCINNATI, OHIO

20 19 18 17 16   5 4 3 2 1

Distributed in Canada by Fraser Direct
100 Armstrong Avenue
Georgetown, ON, Canada L7G 5S4
Tel: (905) 877-4411

Distributed in the U.K. and Europe by F&W MEDIA INTERNATIONAL
Brunel House, Newton Abbot, Devon, TQ12 4PU, England
Tel: (+44) 1626 323200, Fax: (+44) 1626 323319
E-mail: enquiries@fwmedia.com

SRN: S8738
ISBN-13: 978-1-4402-4632-6

PDF SRN: S8743
PDF ISBN-13: 9781440246371

fw

a content + ecommerce company

Editor: Jodi Butler

Technical Editor: Linda Turner Griepentrog

Designer: Elisabeth Lariviere

Photographer: Daniel Cronin

Illustrator: Missy Shepler

CONTENTS

INTRODUCTION

I am a life-long lover of the *Little House* books by Laura Ingalls Wilder. As a "Laura" with sisters myself, I felt kinship with little Half-Pint and often daydreamed about living in her world. The appeal of these wonderful books has stayed with me to this day. When I sit down with one and start reading, I'm transported to a place where belongings are few but cherished and cared for, and where the pace of life allows time to admire the beauty of a wood floor in the sunshine. The combination of adventure, hardship, unspoiled nature, and pride of accomplishment that fills these books has always left me refreshed and contented.

Because of this, I've long thought of making some quilts that I could wrap myself up in and that would remind me of the characters and events that have brought me so many happy hours. So when Andover Fabrics came out with their Little House on the Prairie collections, I was inspired finally to make my imagined quilts. It was so exciting when I finished the first quilt, and it looked like it came right out of the American prairie of the 1860s! There's nothing like having the right colors, prints, and aesthetic when you're trying to bring a certain feeling to a quilt. The vast majority of the fabrics in this book are from these collections. I did throw in a few fabrics from my stash once in a while, but they're few and far between.

Wishing you much joy with your quilts, and with the books of Laura Ingalls Wilder.

—Laura

P.S. Ma, Mary, Laura, and Carrie loved fabric as much as we do!

USING THIS BOOK

BUYING FABRIC

Fabric requirements are based on a usable width of 40 to 42 inches (101.6 to 106.7 centimeters). If wider fabric is necessary, it will be noted in the instructions. The yardage given includes an additional 10 percent to account for uneven cuts when purchasing, shrinkage when prewashing and drying, and individual differences in cutting. Binding yardage is based on using strips 2¼" (5.7 cm) wide and piecing them together with diagonal seams when preparing the binding. Always remove selvages before cutting patches and strips. For best results, use high-quality 100 percent quilters' cottons for the projects in this book (see Choosing and Preparing Fabrics in Chapter 1).

CUTTING AND TEMPLATES

Please cut your strips and patches in the order they're listed. By cutting the pieces that require the full width of the fabric first, followed by the largest patches and strips, you are sure of being able to cut all the patches and strips from the given yardage. All cutting measurements for patches and strips include a ¼" (6 mm) seam allowance. A ¼" (6 mm) seam allowance is also included on templates where required. Appliqué templates are printed reversed and without seam allowances for use with paper-backed fusible web. If you wish to use hand-appliqué, reverse the template, trace your stitching line around the template, then add a seam allowance.

FINISHED SIZES AND SEAM ALLOWANCES

The finished quilt size is the size of the quilt before quilting. The finished block size is the size of a block when sewn into the completed quilt. For example, before being sewn into the quilt, a 12" (30.5 cm) block will be 12½" (31.5 cm) square because of the seam allowances. Please read through each pattern and check the width of your seam allowance using the technique outlined in An Accurate ¼" (6 mm) Seam in Chapter 1 before beginning a project.

DECODING DIAGRAMS

A dotted line across a diagram indicates a fold line (**FIGURE 1**). When looking at the appliqué templates, a dashed line indicates where one template is placed beneath another. Trace the bottom template along the dashed line where it underlays the other template (**FIGURE 2**).

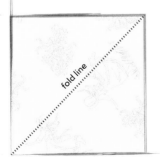

FIGURE 1

FIGURE 2

Chapter 1

QUILTMAKING BASICS AND TECHNIQUES

When Laura Ingalls was making quilts she didn't have the same fabulous tools we do. In her day, patch shapes were drawn in pencil on fabric, then cut out with scissors. The sewing machine was a new and expensive invention, so the Ingalls' quilts were handpieced and handquilted. Both of those techniques are covered in this section, but so are modern practices like rotary cutting and fusible appliqué.

Whether you're a novice or an expert, I hope you'll find something in this section that will make you a better quilter. And it's perfectly fine to use any technique that works for you… beautiful quilts are made in all kinds of ways! Just rest assured that everything you need to know to make the quilts in this book is included here or in the patterns.

BASIC SUPPLIES

Must-haves for every quilter:

- Steam iron and sturdy ironing board with a clean cover (stains can transfer to new fabrics)

- 45 mm rotary cutter and 18" × 24" (45.7 cm × 61 cm) mat

- Acrylic rotary-cutting rulers: 6" × 24" (15.2 cm × 61 cm), 12" (30.5 cm) square, and 6" (15.2 cm) square

- Sewing machine in good working order (Note: If you haven't used it for a couple of years, take it in for a cleaning and a tune-up.)

- A dual-feed feature or a walking foot (makes it easier to sew patches together with precision)

- 100% cotton, low-lint thread (40 or 50 weight) in colors to match your fabrics

- Fabric scissors (don't let them cut paper)

- Snips or small sharp scissors

- Paper scissors

- Awl (for holding the last bit of fabric as it goes under the presser foot)

- Seam ripper

- New, easy-to-pick-up pins and a pincushion (I prefer a magnetic pincushion, but if you have a computerized machine, don't let them get near each other)

- Starch alternative, such as Mary Ellen's Best Press

- Removable marking tool (see Marking the Quilt Top for Quilting in this chapter)

CHOOSING AND PREPARING FABRICS

I recommend using only 100 percent cotton fabric in your quilts. Quilters' cottons should have a dense weave and a minimum of nubs. Beware of fabrics that have been weighted with finishes to mimic higher-quality material. Steer clear of fabric if it feels crunchy, you can see through it, or you can easily see individual threads. For reference, go to the fabric store and do a side-by-side comparison between bolts of the most and least expensive cotton prints. You'll see and feel the difference.

Washing, drying, and pressing fabrics before using them has many benefits. Removing added finishes and chemicals used in the manufacturing process is important for those with sensitive skin, as well as for children and pets. I prefer to use a starch alternative when pressing fabric because it doesn't attract insects. If you use starch, wash any leftover fabric before adding it to your stash.

HALF-PINT TIP
Cutting and Measuring

Don't use a rotary cutter if you're tired, don't have enough light, or are distracted. Close the cutter after every cut. If you need to press hard to cut the fabric, change the blade. And (really) measure twice before cutting. It'll save you a lot of grief.

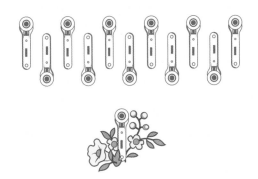

CUTTING ACCURATELY

After being cut at the store, washed, dried, and ironed, fabric is rarely straight. You must start with a straight edge across the width of your fabric that is perpendicular to the selvages. To do this, bring the selvage edges together and allow the fabric to drop in front of you (**FIGURE 1**). Keeping the selvages even, slide the edges sideways with your fingers until the fabric falls straight with no skewing. Now lay the fabric on the cutting mat with the fold toward you and the raw edge to be straightened to the right (or to the left if you're left-handed). Place a 6" × 24" (15.2 cm × 61 cm) rotary-cutting ruler on the fabric, aligning one of the horizontal lines precisely along the fold. Press down firmly on the ruler with your left (right) hand and, keeping the blade upright and against the ruler's edge, roll the cutter away from you while applying gentle pressure (**FIGURE 2**). You can cut part of the way, stop cutting without lifting the cutter, then move your ruler hand further up on the ruler before finishing the cut.

- **To cut strips,** place the newly-straightened edge to your left (right) and then find the line on the ruler that corresponds to the width of strip you want to cut. Position the ruler so this line exactly aligns with the cut edge and then cut the strip (**FIGURE 3**).

- **To cut squares,** stack 1 or more strips of the same width, aligning edges (**FIGURE 4**). Align a horizontal line on the ruler with the edges and cut across to create ends perpendicular to the strips. Now cut across the strips, making cuts the same width as the strips.

- **To cut half-square triangles from a square,** place the square on the mat and position the rotary-cutting ruler diagonally so that the edge goes through opposite corners of the square. Cut across the square (**FIGURE 5**).

- **To cut quarter-square triangles,** make 2 diagonal cuts across the square, without moving the triangles after the first cut (**FIGURE 6**)

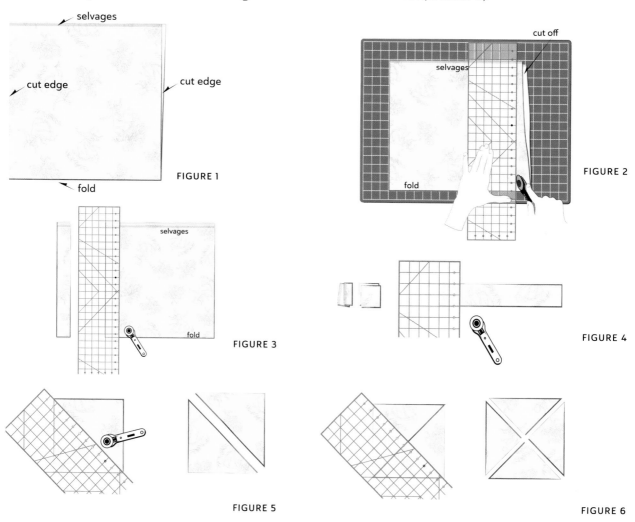

FIGURE 1

FIGURE 2

FIGURE 3

FIGURE 4

FIGURE 5

FIGURE 6

MACHINE PIECING

Layer two patches right sides together with the raw edges aligned, then insert pins perpendicular to the seam (**FIGURE 7**). Remove the pins just before they reach the needle.

An accurate ¼" (6 mm) seam allowance is critical (for tips, see An Accurate ¼" [6 mm] Seam). A ¼" (6 mm) presser foot is available for most sewing machines. You can also place a piece of painter's tape or set a pad of sticky notes on your sewing machine ¼" (6 mm) to the right of the needle. When stitching, align the raw edges of the fabric with the tape or sticky notes.

A machine-stitched seam is usually sewn from raw edge to raw edge. Backstitching isn't necessary if the seam will be crossed by another line of stitching later. Backstitching is recommended for seams that are on the outermost edge of the quilt.

HAND PIECING

Place a template right-side down on the wrong side of the fabric, aligning the grain line on the template with the fabric grain (**FIGURE 8**). Trace around the edge of the template; this is your sewing line. Cut out the fabric patch, adding approximately ¼" (6 mm) on all sides for the seam allowance.

Place two patches right sides together, aligning the seam lines. Insert pins through the layered fabrics near each end of the seam and every 1½" (3.8 cm) in between.

Using an unknotted 18" (45.7 cm) long thread, take a stitch and a backstitch on the seam line, beginning at the marked corner (not on the fabric edge). Make small, evenly spaced running stitches on the seam line, backstitching at the end of the seam (**FIGURE 9**). Don't stitch into the seam allowances. Trim the thread, then open your newly-sewn unit and finger press the seam allowances toward the darker fabric or in the direction where there are fewer seams. Don't press with an iron until your block is complete.

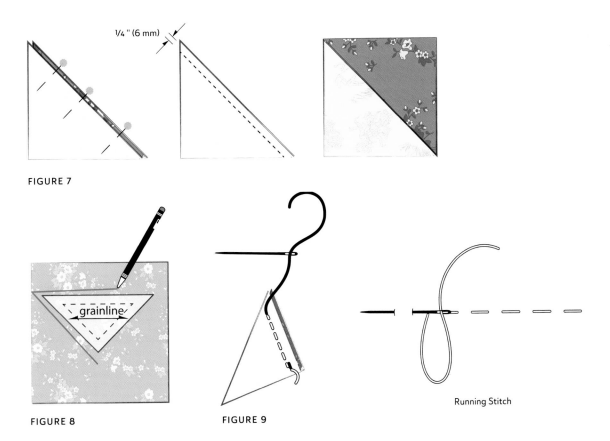

¼ " (6 mm)

FIGURE 7

grainline

FIGURE 8

FIGURE 9

Running Stitch

AN ACCURATE ¼" (6 MM) SEAM

Inaccurate cutting and inaccurate seam allowances are the most common reasons why quilters run into problems. Seam allowances can vary, even if you have a ¼" (6 mm) presser foot. Also, when seams are opened and pressed, a bit of fabric can be left in the seam, which can leave you with units that are too small. Even a small inaccuracy in seam width can make a big difference. For example, if an allowance is off by ¹⁄₁₆" (1.6 mm), and there are 8 seams in the block or unit, that block or unit will be off by ½" (1.3 cm). It adds up fast!

If you find that your sewn units aren't coming together properly, one of the following may be the reason why:

- You're not using a fine, low-lint thread in both the top of your machine and in the bobbin. Thick thread can cause units with multiple seams to be too small.

- You're not pressing seams flat to set the stitching before pressing seams open or you're not pressing the seams completely open (see Pressing).

- Your seam guide isn't properly positioned.

If these things seem to be fine, your seam allowances may be too wide or too narrow.

To find out if your seam allowances are truly ¼" (6 mm), try this seam allowance test. Cut (3) 1½" × 4½" (3.8 cm × 11.4 cm) strips. Using the same guide, sew 2 of the patches together along their long edge. Press as usual, then add the third strip in the same manner and press. Measure the sewn unit. It should be exactly 3½" (8.9 cm) wide from raw edge to raw edge if your seams are pressed completely open. If the unit is wider than 3½" (8.9 cm), move your guide farther away from the needle. If the unit is narrower than 3½" (8.9 cm), move the guide closer to the needle and try again. Repeat this test until you are consistently sewing an accurate ¼" (6 mm) seam.

PRESSING

One of the most important parts of successful quilt-making is proper pressing. Iron freshly washed fabric with steam, moving the iron back and forth as you would when ironing a garment. Use a spray finish or a starch alternative when ironing fabric that will be cut on the bias. It makes the fabric firmer and less likely to stretch when handled.

When piecing, press after sewing each seam. Use a light touch and a dry iron when pressing seams. Always set each seam by pressing it flat before you press it open. This helps the thread integrate with the fabric. When pressing a seam open, use your hand to open the piece to be pressed, then place the iron down on the seam. Lift the iron to move it farther down the seam, continuing to open the seam with your hand. Don't push the iron back and forth as this can distort the unit you're pressing. Be especially careful when working with strip sets. It's easy for the pressed strip set to curve, instead of laying straight. Try pressing from opposite ends of the strip set with each strip added. When you're working with bias edges, press them as little as possible before they are sewn to another piece.

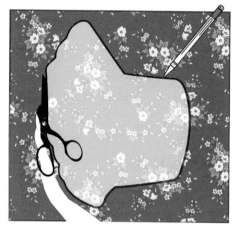

FIGURE 10

NEEDLE-TURN APPLIQUÉ

Place the template right-side up on the right side of the fabric. Using a tool that makes removable marks, lightly draw around the template. Cut out the shape, adding a ¼" (6 mm) seam allowance on all sides for most shapes or an ⅛" (3 mm) seam allowance for small shapes (FIGURE 10).

To blindstitch the appliqué shapes, position the shape on the background fabric and secure it in place with a pin or a dab of washable glue stick. Select a coordinating thread color (100 percent cotton thread will be less visible than a cotton/polyester blend).

Begin stitching on a straight or gently curved edge, not at a sharp point or corner. Turn under a short length of the seam allowance using your fingers and the point of the needle until the drawn seam line is just barely turned under. With a knotted thread no more than 18" (45.7 cm) long, come up through the backing fabric and catch just one or two threads on the edge of the appliqué shape. At the edge of the appliqué, push the needle back down through the background fabric only, just next to the point at which the thread emerges from the appliqué shape. Moving about ⅛" (3 mm) from the first stitch, come up again through both the background fabric and the appliqué shape, again catching one or two threads on the edge of the appliqué shape before inserting the needle into the background fabric as before (**FIGURE 11**). Note: The thread should be visible on the wrong side of the block, but almost invisible on the right side.

As you stitch around the edge of the appliqué piece, use your fingers and the point of the needle to turn under the seam allowance as you go. When the shape has been completely stitched in place, knot off the thread on the wrong side of the fabric.

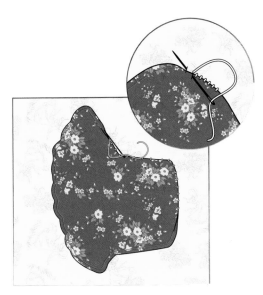

FIGURE 11

DIRECTIONAL FABRICS

Directional fabrics are those printed with a design that has an obvious orientation to it. An example of this is the prairie print from the Little House collection. The houses, grass, and clouds make it obvious which way is the right-side up. Stripes are another type of directional fabric (I've used them to make the side and roof of the house in the Big Sky quilt look like it was made of logs). When working with directional fabrics, it's crucial to pay attention to grainline directions in the cutting instructions to get the look you want.

CHAIN-PIECING

Chain-piecing is a way to speed up the piecing process when you're sewing multiples of the same unit. Start by pairing up patches that are to be sewn together and aligning them right sides together. Stack the paired patches within easy reach, next to your sewing machine. Feeding one pair after another under the presser foot, sew the units together without cutting the threads between them. After stitching the first pair, take a few stitches without any fabric under the needle; then insert the second pair. The sewing threads form short chains between the sewn pairs. Continue in this manner until all the paired patches have been stitched. Cut the chains to separate the pairs before pressing.

HALF-PINT TIP

Sharpen Your Shears

Want to get your best scissors sharpened by an expert? Ask your hair stylist for the name and number of the person who sharpens his or her shears.

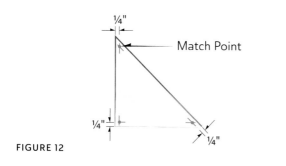

FIGURE 12

FIGURE 13   **FIGURE 14**

FIGURE 15

FIGURE 16

FIGURE 17

MATCH POINTS

Match points are used to position patches correctly before sewing them together. Sometimes it's hard to see how two patches should be aligned as they go through the machine.

It's easy to add match points to any patch. On the wrong side of the patch, use a see-through acrylic ruler to draw a short line ¼" (6 mm) from each raw edge at the corners. The places where the lines cross are the match points (**FIGURE 12**).

To use match points, place the patches right sides together. Insert a pin through the center of one match point and then through the corresponding match point on the other patch (**FIGURE 13**). Keeping the pin perpendicular to the fabrics and holding the fabrics together, place a pin to either side of the first pin (**FIGURE 14**). Remove the first pin.

FUSSY-CUTTING

Fussy-cutting is when a patch is cut so that a specific motif or section of the fabric is showcased within the block. This can be a flower centered in each square of a Nine Patch block or a triangle cut so that stripes run perpendicular to its long side. For examples, see the Big Sky quilt. A common use of fussy-cutting is when you want to use a specific part of a panel or large print. The possibilities are endless!

Start by drawing the size and shape of the patch on see-through template plastic material, marking the seam allowances (**FIGURE 15**). Cut out the plastic template. Place the template on the right side of the fabric so that the chosen motif is positioned within the shape as desired, remembering that the fabric outside the seam allowance lines will not show in the finished block (**FIGURE 16**). Trace around the template, then cut out on the drawn lines (**FIGURE 17**).

DIY APPLIQUÉ TEMPLATES
Heat-Resistant Template Plastic

Heat-resistant template plastic is most commonly used to prepare appliqué shapes for hand-appliqué. To make a template, place the plastic over the template pattern and trace around the shape with a fine-point permanent marker. Cut out the template, then transfer any notes from the pattern, including the quilt name,

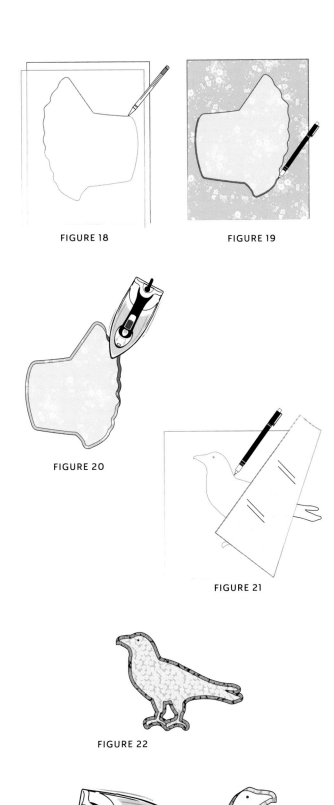

FIGURE 18

FIGURE 19

FIGURE 20

FIGURE 21

FIGURE 22

FIGURE 23

template letter, and placement lines, to the right side of the template (**FIGURE 18**).

Place the template right-side down on the wrong side of the fabric and trace around it using a mechanical pencil (**FIGURE 19**). Cut out the traced shape about ¼" (6 mm) beyond the traced line for the seam allowance. Center the plastic template on the wrong side of the fabric shape. Being careful not to burn your fingers, use a dry iron to press the seam allowances over the edge of the plastic (**FIGURE 20**). To make a crisp edge that stays in place while you're appliquéing, brush liquid starch or starch alternative on the seam allowance before pressing it over the template edge. Let the template cool, then remove it and use the template again to make as many shapes as required.

Freezer Paper

Freezer paper is a godsend to quilters. It has two sides, a shiny side and a matte side. The shiny side has a wax coating that allows a template to temporarily adhere to fabric while leaving no residue behind. To make a freezer paper template, place the freezer paper shiny side down on the printed template pattern. Trace the shape with a pencil or fine-point pen, then cut out the template on the line and transfer any notes from the pattern to the right side of the template, including the quilt name, template letter, and any placement lines (**FIGURE 21**).

Use a dry iron to press the freezer paper, shiny side down, to the right side of the fabric. Leaving the freezer paper template in place, cut out the fabric shape ¼" (6 mm) beyond the template for the seam allowance (**FIGURE 22**). Peel off the freezer paper and center it, matte side down, on the wrong side of the fabric shape. Using a dry iron, press the seam allowance over the edge of the freezer paper, holding it in place for a second or two until it adheres to the paper (**FIGURE 23**). Be careful not to get your fingers too close to the iron. Leaving the freezer paper in place, position the appliqué on the background fabric. Using a dry iron, press the appliqué to the background fabric, holding the iron in place a second or two until the freezer paper adheres to the background fabric

FIGURE 24

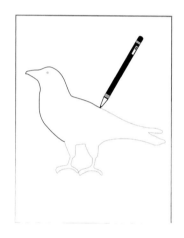

FIGURE 25

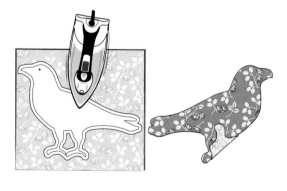

FIGURE 26

(**FIGURE 24**). Hand- or machine stitch the shape in place, removing the freezer paper when you've sewn almost around the entire shape. Or finish appliquéing the shape in place, then carefully cut a small slit through the background fabric only beneath the center of the appliqué, and then remove the paper through the slit (there's no need to sew the slit closed).

Paper-Backed Fusible Web

Paper-backed fusible web has a paper side and a textured side. The textured side has a form of heat-activated fabric adhesive. There are several brands of paper-backed fusible web on the market. For quilting, light- to medium-weight is best (heavyweight fusible web can make quilts feel stiff). Always follow the manufacturer's instructions when fusing.

When using fusible web, you need to trace a reversed pattern. Because the fusible web shape is turned over when being appliquéd, it's important to use a pattern that has already been reversed or to trace the shape from the wrong side of the pattern. To do that, turn your printed pattern over and use a permanent pen to trace the shape on the back of the paper (**FIGURE 25**). If your printer has a reverse function, simply copy the pattern with the reverse option selected.

When you have a reversed pattern shape, trace it onto the paper side of the fusible web. Or you can use an ink-jet printer to print on most paper-backed webs. Just cut the fusible web into 8½" × 11" (21.6 cm × 28 cm) rectangles, then load them one at a time into the paper tray of the printer in the correct orientation for the printing to appear on the paper side of the sheet.

Cut out the template, leaving a small margin beyond the drawn lines. You don't have to be precise. Fuse the template to the wrong side of the fabric, following the manufacturer's instructions. Cut out the shape on the drawn line (**FIGURE 26**). Position the shape on the background fabric and fuse it in place. Using a sewing machine, edgestitch the appliqué to secure it. For large shapes, cut away most of the fusible web from the center of the shape before fusing, leaving a ½" (1.3 cm) margin inside the drawn line. This way, the appliqué will remain soft and pliable after fusing. Fuse this window-like shape to the wrong side of the fabric and cut it out on the drawn line.

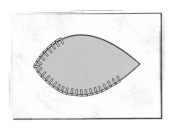

Blanket Stitch

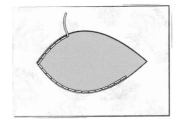

Straight Stitch

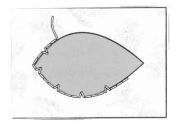

Blind Hem Stitch

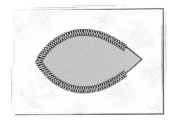

Satin Stitch

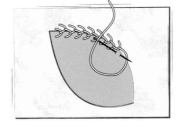

Feather Stitch

FIGURE 27

EDGESTITCHING APPLIQUÉ

After fusing an appliqué shape in place, it's important to secure the edges with some type of stitching (**FIGURE 27**). My favorite way is to use a machine blanket stitch or another pretty decorative stitch (my machine has a fabulous leafy vine stitch) and matching thread. You can use other machine stitches and threads as well. A simple machine straight stitch approximately ⅛" (3 mm) in from the edge of the appliqué is a good choice, as is a blind hem stitch. If using the blind hem stitch, make sure that the "swing" part of the stitch reaches approximately an ⅛" (3 mm) into the appliqué.

Some quilters prefer to use a machine satin stitch to secure the edge. A satin stitch is a zigzag stitch with the stitches very close together (a stitch length of almost zero) that straddles the edge of the appliqué. I recommend using some sort of stabilizer under the appliqué when satin stitching, to prevent tunneling. You can also use pearl cotton or floss with a hand blanket stitch, hand feather stitch, or another embroidery stitch. Whichever stitch you use, be sure to pull the beginning and ending threads (both top thread and bobbin thread) to the back of the quilt top, knot them off, then dab them with the tiniest bit of a seam sealant, such as Fray Check, so they can't ravel.

HALF-PINT TIP
Low-Cost Backings

I was told not to use sheets for quilt backs because they can be densely woven and hard to handquilt through. Since most of my quilts are machine-quilted, I don't have a problem getting a needle through the finish that many sheets have. When buying sheets with a thread count of 200 or less, I always check the density. If the sheet feels like a quilters' cotton and I can't see through it, then I buy it and wash it. When it comes out of the dryer, I check the fabric again to make sure the density matches my quilt top fabric. I've found 100 percent cotton sheets on sale that have made great backs.

FOUNDATION PAPER PIECING

Foundation paper piecing makes it possible to stitch odd angles and shapes without having to make templates. I like the method that uses the Add-A-Quarter ruler from Carolyn McCormick, with a few additions. You'll need an Add-A-Quarter ruler (available online and at quilt stores), an index card or piece of template plastic with a straight edge, and a washable glue stick.

First, make copies of the foundation masters you are using from the same original and on the same copier. To check the accuracy of the first copy, hold the original and the copy together with a light source behind them. If there's no skewing or size change, make as many copies as needed on the lightest weight paper possible (you can buy paper made for this purpose). After making copies, trim each shape leaving ⅛-¼" (3-6 mm) on all sides. Do not trim on the line.

Set the stitch length on your sewing machine to 18-20 stitches per inch. The smaller stitches make it easier to remove the paper later.

Take a look at the foundation master (**FIGURE 28**). The lines indicate where to sew and the numbers indicate the sequence in which to sew. The only seam allowances shown are the ones that go around a block or unit. The lines and numbers are printed on the front of the pattern (the side you sew on), while the back is blank and goes against the fabric.

1. Place the appropriate patch for area 1 on the blank side of the foundation master, making sure the patch extends beyond the area lines by at least ¼" (6 mm) on all sides; use a tiny dab of washable glue stick to hold it in place. Turn the foundation and fabric over. Align the edge of the index card on the sewing line between areas 1 and 2 (**FIGURE 29**). Fold back the foundation over the edge of the index card (you will see fabric beyond the paper). Place the Add-A-Quarter ruler up against the fold of the foundation paper lip-side down, then use a rotary cutter to trim the excess fabric from the patch (**FIGURE 30**). You will now have a straight line to help you position the next patch.

2. Unfold the foundation and turn it over. Place the patch for area 2 right-side down on the area 1 patch, aligning one edge of the second patch with the newly trimmed edge of the area 1 patch (**FIGURE 31**). Holding the second patch in place, turn the paper over and stitch on the line between areas 1 and 2, extending the seam by a few stitches at each end (**FIGURE 32**). Flip the paper over and open the second patch (**FIGURE 33**). Press with a dry iron.

3. Fold the foundation paper back over the index card along the next line to be sewn, which in this case is the line between areas 1 and 3. Butt the ruler up against the paper and trim the excess fabric (**FIGURE 34**). In the same manner as before, turn the foundation over and align one edge of an area 3 patch with the newly trimmed edge of the area 1 patch (**FIGURE 35**). Sew on the line between areas 1 and 3 (**FIGURE 36**), and then open and press as before (**FIGURE 37**).

4. In the same manner, continue sewing each patch in place in the numeric order given until the unit is complete. Trim the edges on the solid lines to create a ¼" (6mm) seam allowance (**FIGURE 38**). Do not remove the paper from the unit until step 6.

5. If you are paper piecing a block that is made up of multiple units, sew them together now. If you have points that need to match, carefully push a positioning pin straight through a match point on the top unit. Then, with right sides together and edges aligned, push the pin straight through the corresponding match point on the second unit. Leaving the positioning pin vertical, pin as normal to either side of the positioning pin, then remove it. Pin the rest of the seam as usual. Sew the pieced units together as if they were ordinary fabric patches (**FIGURE 39**), removing pins just before they reach the needle of your machine.

6. When the block is finished, do not remove the paper. Join the blocks to the rest of the quilt first. This gives you a line to follow when sewing the blocks together and the paper helps to keep the integrity of the block. Remove the paper after the blocks are sewn together. A pair of tweezers can be used to remove the tiniest pieces of paper, but it's better to leave a little paper in the seam than to pull on stitches. (Tiny pieces will dissolve when the quilt is washed.) If you're having trouble, mist the back of the block and let it sit for a few minutes before trying again. Before misting, make sure to test this on a scrap of the lightest fabric in the quilt to make sure the ink doesn't transfer.

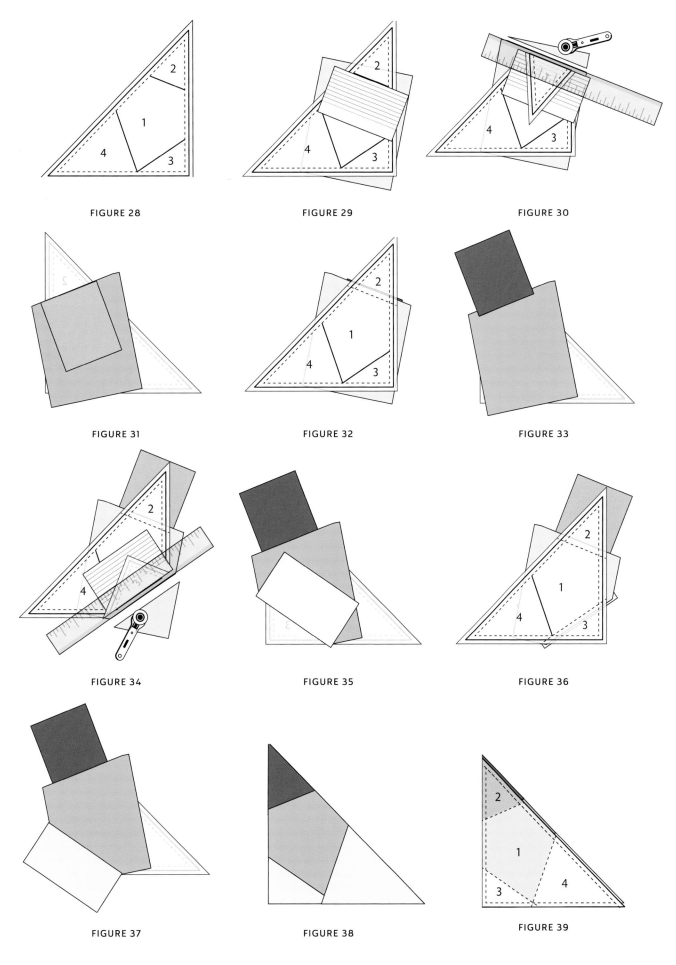

FIGURE 28

FIGURE 29

FIGURE 30

FIGURE 31

FIGURE 32

FIGURE 33

FIGURE 34

FIGURE 35

FIGURE 36

FIGURE 37

FIGURE 38

FIGURE 39

ASSEMBLY

Quilt-top assembly is usually addressed in pattern instructions, but these good practices can make a big difference in the final appearance of the quilt.

- Press the quilt top carefully during assembly, using an up-and-down motion with the iron rather than pushing it along. Always press on the wrong side first so the seam allowances lie flat, then press the front. If the seams aren't fully open and there's a little tuck of fabric along a seam line, pressing on the right side helps you see where this happened so you can fix it.

- Square up a quilt before adding borders. First, measure the pressed quilt lengthwise and width-wise three times as shown (**FIGURE 40**). Ideally, the three measurements will be within about a ½" (1.3 cm) of each other. If they are, consider the quilt top square and use the average of the three measurements to determine the length of the border strips. (To find the average, add the three measurements together, then divide by 3.) If the measurements aren't close to one another, look at the last seams sewn to see if they were pressed fully open. Are these last seam allowances too wide or too narrow along one edge? If so, unsew a ways and fix the seams. If there's still a big difference, check the blocks for errors. However, some quilts are made to be loved, and no one will care if the borders are uneven, lumps can't be quilted out, or the corners aren't square. If this is the quilt you're making, you may decide that finished is better than perfect. If you want your quilt to be closer to perfect but don't want to resew blocks, you can do a little trimming. This is a last resort. Trimming can change the look of a quilt and not always in a good way. If you decide to trim, trim only until the difference in measurements is down to about ¼" (6 mm). Use the same measuring and trimming process, if needed, with each border you add.

- Always backstitch seam ends on the perimeter of the quilt top so that they don't come undone when the quilt is being quilted.

ADDING MITERED BORDERS

To add mitered borders to a quilt, center and pin the border strips to the sides, top, and bottom of the quilt. The strips will extend beyond the quilt top. Starting

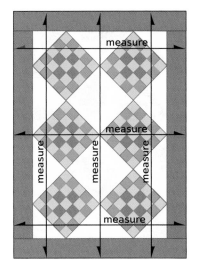

FIGURE 40

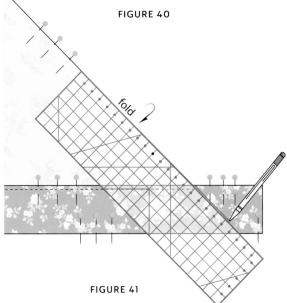

FIGURE 41

and stopping ¼" (6 mm) from the quilt corners and backstitching to secure, sew the borders to the quilt center. Press the seam allowances toward the quilt center. Fold the quilt on the diagonal, right sides together. Align the border strip raw edges and the border seams at the ¼" (6 mm) backstitched point and pin them together. Align the edge of a ruler with the fold, extending the ruler completely across the border. Draw a line from the backstitched point to the raw edges (**FIGURE 41**). Stitch the border strips together on the drawn line, backstitching at both ends. Press the seam open. With the quilt right-side up, align the 45° angle line of a square ruler on the seam line to check for accuracy. If the corner is flat and square, trim the excess fabric to a ¼" (6 mm) seam allowance. Repeat on the remaining corners.

BACKINGS

Backing fabric should be of the same quality as the quilt top fabric, which means 100 percent cotton with a tight weave. If the weave of the backing fabric is looser than the weave of the quilt top fabrics, the backing may shrink more than the top when the quilt is washed, causing the quilt to permanently bunch up.

A quilt backing must be at least 4" (10.2 cm) larger than the top on all sides if it's going to be quilted by a longarm quilter. Even if it is handquilted, having 4" (10.2 cm) extra on all sides is preferable.

Extra-wide yardage is available for quilt backings, so you may not need to piece your backing. If you use a 40" (101.6 cm) wide fabric for a quilt larger than 32" (81.3 cm) square, you will need to piece the backing. I use a ½" (1.3 cm) seam allowance when piecing backings and press the seams open.

BATTING

Like the backing, the batting in a quilt needs to be at least 4" (10.2 cm) larger than the top on all sides. There are other factors to consider as well when choosing batting. Do you want a puffy quilt or a flat quilt? How will it be quilted? How much quilting will there be? What is your budget? How will the quilt be used? There are many types of batting. Here are some things to look for:

- Content (fibers used, whether or not chemicals or resins have been added, if it's eco-friendly)
- Size
- Loft (how flat or puffy the batting is)
- Cost
- Warmth level
- Breathability
- Washability
- Weight
- Durability
- How closely it needs to be quilted or tied
- Color: natural, white, black, gray (to prevent show-through, use a white batting if the quilt surface is predominately light, and a dark batting if the quilt is mostly dark).

Batting fiber content:

- **100 percent cotton batting** is my favorite. I love the way a quilt with cotton batting looks after being washed and dried. The batting shrinks a bit to give a quilt that old-fashioned, slightly rumpled look. It is also durable, breathable, and has a nice weight. Cotton batting should be quilted no more than 8" (20.3 cm) apart, depending on the brand.
- **Polyester batting** has a lighter weight than cotton batting and is very soft, especially for handquilting. Because it doesn't breathe like natural fibers, it can make a quilt very warm. It's also less expensive than other battings. However, it burns at a lower temperature than any natural fiber and can melt, which makes it a poor choice for a child's quilt.
- **Bamboo batting** is softer than cotton batting and has a unique antibacterial quality. It breathes well and has good moisture absorption, so it is especially good for a summer quilt. When combined with cotton, bamboo softens batting and creates a lighter quilt with a somewhat old-fashioned look.
- **Soy and cotton** are now available blended together in a batting that is soft, durable, breathable, and resists bearding. Because it's relatively new, we don't know how it will last over decades.
- **Fire-resistant battings**, often made of rayon, are permanently fire-resistant. Rayon is breathable and soft yet retains warmth, making it the ultimate batting for a baby quilt.
- **An 80 percent cotton / 20 percent polyester blend** batting is soft and durable. The polyester makes the batting lighter in weight than an all-cotton batting, and the quilting can be farther apart. It also costs slightly less than cotton batting.
- **Wool battings** are expensive but wonderful. They are naturally fire-resistant, relatively lightweight, machine-washable, and breathe well. If you want your quilting to stand out, wool is a good choice.

Battings are also available in silk, Tencel, and even fibers made from recycled plastic bottles. Try different battings over time to discover what you like best.

MARKING THE QUILT TOP FOR QUILTING

Before layering and basting a quilt, you'll want to mark it for quilting, unless you're taking it to a longarmer. After the quilt top has been pressed and squared up, choose a marking tool that makes a thin accurate line. Options include water-soluble or air-erasable markers, marking pencils, white dressmaker's pencils, chalk pencils, chalk rolling markers, and slivers of hardened soap. Try using silver and yellow Berol pencils on dark fabrics or a No. 4 pencil sparingly on light fabric. The same project may need several types of markers. Read the instructions for your chosen marking tool and test anything you plan to use on fabric scraps first, to make sure it comes off and stays off. Some water- or air-erasable markers can become permanent if exposed to heat, such as from an iron or being left in a hot car.

Reduce or enlarge quilting designs on a photocopier to fit your border or block. To transfer a design, try one of these techniques:

- Trace quilting designs onto light-colored fabric using a light box or a glass-top table with a light underneath. Darken the lines on the photocopy with a permanent pen, if they're difficult to see.
- Punch holes in the paper photocopy along the design outlines. Lay the paper on dark fabric, then sprinkle powdered chalk or cornstarch on the paper. When you're done, gently lift the paper and connect the dots with a marking tool.
- Use a stencil to mark your quilt. You can make plastic stencils with stencil-making tools. Or draw a shape on freezer paper, cut it out, press it to the quilt top, and quilt around it. Cookie cutters, coins, and rulers can also be used to mark a quilt.

LAYERING

Layering and basting are much easier when you have someone to help you. So plan your layering and basting session for a time when a friend is available.

First, read the batting package to see if you should lay the batting out to relax before layering. Press the backing and the top. Place the backing wrong-side up on a smooth flat surface larger than the quilt. Smooth out any wrinkles and, if possible, use painter's tape to hold the backing taut to the work surface. Center the batting on the backing and smooth out any wrinkles gently so that you don't create wrinkles in the backing. Now, carefully place the quilt top in the center of the batting and gently smooth it out. Make sure you have at least 4" (10.2 cm) of batting and backing beyond the top on every side. Use straight pins to keep the layers from shifting while you baste (**FIGURE 42**).

If you don't have a large smooth surface that isn't carpeted, try this. Smooth out the backing as before, but pin the edges to the carpet itself. Add the batting

and quilt top in the same manner, but before pinning the layers together, grab a cutting mat. Remove a few pins along the edge of the backing and slide your cutting mat under the quilt sandwich. Replace most of the pins, leaving an opening for your hand. Pin the area above the mat, then slide the mat over and pin the next area. Continue to remove and replace pins on the edge as you slide the mat along. Use the mat in the same way when basting. **Note:** If your quilt is going to be quilted by a longarmer there is no need to layer or baste the quilt.

BASTING

The purpose of basting is to hold the layers together so they don't shift during quilting. It's important to baste securely. A poorly basted quilt will have puckers and wrinkles on the back. To baste a quilt for handquilting, thread a darning needle with a piece of thread (in a neutral color) that is about 12" (30.5 cm) longer than the quilt. Leaving the thread unknotted, begin in the center of the quilt and stitch toward the top, using a 1½" (3.8 cm) long running stitch to baste the layers together (**FIGURE 43**). Baste from the center to the top edge, then take a backstitch or two in the batting and backing beyond the quilt top to secure the thread. Unthread the needle. Half the thread should still be lying on the quilt top near where you began. Thread the needle with this thread and, in the same manner, use a running stitch to baste the quilt in the opposite direction (**FIGURE 44**). The second line of basting should be from edge to edge across the horizontal center. Continue to baste in a grid or starburst pattern until the layers are completely stabilized (**FIGURE 45**).

Pin-basting is used when machine quilting. Use only nickel-plated safety pins, to prevent rust stains. Start in the center of the quilt and use a safety pin to pin through all three layers. Place a pin about every 4" (10.2 cm), working in a circular pattern and moving out toward the edges (**FIGURE 46**). While quilting, remove safety pins when they approach the needle.

MACHINE QUILTING

It's possible to get great results with a home machine. You'll need an even-feed or walking foot to ensure quilting a straight line without distorting the layers, and a darning foot for free-motion or heavily curved stitching. A single-hole throat plate is helpful

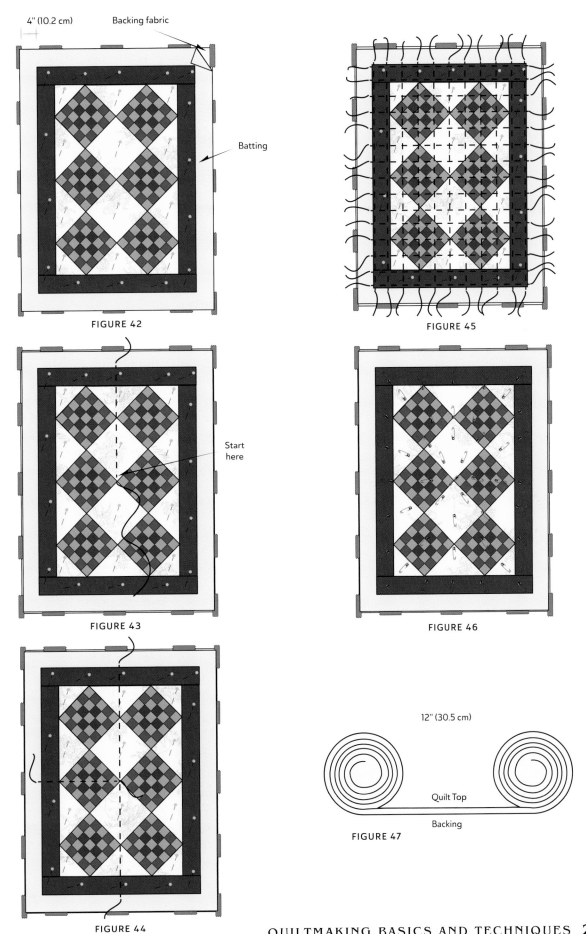

4" (10.2 cm)

Backing fabric

Batting

FIGURE 42

FIGURE 43

Start here

FIGURE 44

FIGURE 45

FIGURE 46

12" (30.5 cm)

Quilt Top

Backing

FIGURE 47

for smooth stitching. If you've never quilted on your machine, layer some practice sandwiches, using a yard of fabric with selvages removed for the backing, a piece of batting the same size as the backing, and a slightly smaller piece of fabric for the top. Pin-baste the layers together.

For straight line stitching, roll both long edges of the quilt toward the center, with the top facing up until there is about a 12" (30.5 cm) wide area between the rolls at the center of the quilt (**FIGURE 47**). As you quilt, work your way to the right, unrolling the right edge as needed. When you've finished the right half of the quilt, roll up the quilted side and place it to your left as you quilt the remaining half of the quilt.

For free-motion quilting, such as meandering and stippling, use a darning foot and lower your machine's feed dogs. Instead of rolling the edges toward the center, slide the center of the quilt under the presser foot and smooth an area to be quilted. Gently bunch up the rest of the quilt around the flat center so it doesn't pull on the working area. Quilt by slowly moving the quilt under the darning foot with your fingertips, keeping your fingers clear of the needle. Try to keep the machine at a steady, medium speed to create even stitches. Stop quilting when necessary to smooth a new area to quilt, rearranging the rest of the quilt so that it doesn't pull on the working area.

HANDQUILTING

Handquilting features evenly spaced, small stitches on both sides of the quilt, with no knots showing on the back. I like using 100 percent cotton quilting thread. If you haven't handquilted before, start with a size 8 or 9 "between" needle and advance to a shorter size 10 or 12 needle for finer stitching. Use a well-fitting,

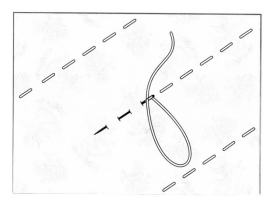

FIGURE 48

puncture-proof thimble on the middle finger of your sewing hand to push the needle through the quilt layers.

Some quilters use a frame or hoop to keep the layered quilt smooth and taut, while others prefer to quilt without one. Try both methods on a practice quilt sandwich to decide which you prefer. Select a comfortable seat with proper back support and a good light source, preferably natural light. To begin, cut a 24" (61 cm) length of thread and make a small knot on one end. On the front of the quilt, place the needle tip either into a seam line or ½" (1.3 cm) behind the point where quilting stitches are to begin, then guide it through the batting and up through the quilt top to "bury" the knot. Gently pull on the thread until you hear the knot "pop" through the quilt top. Trim the thread tail, if needed.

To quilt using a running stitch (**FIGURE 48**), hold the needle parallel to the quilt top and stitch up and down through the three layers with a rocking motion, making several stitches at a time. This technique is called "stacking." Gently and smoothly pull the thread through the layers. To end, make a small knot and bury it in the batting as before, then trim the thread tail.

TYING A QUILT

Tying a quilt is a quick and inexpensive way to turn a quilt top into a quilt. It's not as durable as quilting, but it can still be a fine alternative for a quilt that is meant to be loved. Quilts are usually tied with yarn or embroidery floss. I prefer pearl cotton to floss because the strands don't separate. If you'll be using yarn, I suggest a sock-weight 100 percent cotton yarn. You'll also need a thimble (to push the needle), scissors, and a large needle with a sharp point and an eye large enough for your pearl cotton or yarn. Don't use a tapestry needle, as they are made with blunt points for working on needlepoint canvas. I also suggest using a little seam sealant on every knot.

Decide where you'd like your ties to be. They can be in the middle of a every block or unit, along the seams, or even in a pattern across the quilt (such as diagonal lines). Just be sure to keep the spacing equal in distances that are appropriate for the batting being used. Read the batting label to find out how far apart your ties can be.

Thread the needle with yarn or pearl cotton. It can be tricky threading a needle with a thicker fiber, so try this trick if you're having trouble. Fold one end of a 20–24" (50.8–61 cm) length of yarn or pearl cotton over the needle and pinch. Holding it tightly, remove the needle and push the folded yarn into the needle eye.

Insert the needle down through all three quilt layers, making sure the needle exits through the backing, then bring the needle back up through the three layers, coming out ¼" (6 mm) away from where you started. Pull the yarn through until you have a 2" (5.1 cm) tail (**FIGURE 49**). Keeping the tail out of the way, insert the needle again in the same spot, go down and back up again through all three layers as before, emerging ¼" (6 mm) away from the initial spot again. Cut the yarn or pearl cotton, leaving another 2" (5.1 cm) tail (**FIGURE 50**).

Use a double knot to tie the tails together. Trim the tails to about 1" (2.5 cm) long. Dab a tiny drop of seam sealant into the center of the knot (**FIGURE 51**).

SQUARING UP A QUILT

Once your piece is quilted, you need to make the edges even and square before adding the binding. Before you can do any trimming, sew the layers together at the edge of the quilt. Using a walking foot (also known as an even feed foot) or the dual-feed feature on your sewing machine, zigzag down the very edge of the

outer border with a basting stitch length. Your stitches should be within the ¼" (6 mm) seam allowance so that they will not show once the binding is attached. If you don't have a walking foot, baste the edges by hand right inside the ¼" (6 mm) seam allowance.

After stitching the edge, trim the excess batting and backing. Lay the quilted piece on a cutting mat with the top and one side in position for trimming. If your quilt is larger than your table, support the quilt so that it doesn't pull at the edges.

With the 6" × 24" (15.2 cm × 61 cm) rotary ruler in hand, decide what to use as a guide when cutting. If you have added a border that is narrower than the ruler, use the seam line as your guide when cutting. Line this seam up with a vertical line on the ruler and continue to place the ruler in that same position as you move around the four sides. If your border is wider than the ruler, tape two rulers together side by side. If your quilt doesn't have a border, use a seam line where one column or row of blocks was sewn to another.

Make sure the quilt is flat, then position your ruler with the 24" (61 cm) edge along the side edge of the quilt and the 6" (15.2 cm) side of the ruler aligned with the top of the quilt. This will allow you to trim around the corner at a right angle. Try to cut as little as possible from the quilt top. Instead, trim away the batting and backing so that it aligns with the outermost part of the quilt top while maintaining a constant distance from

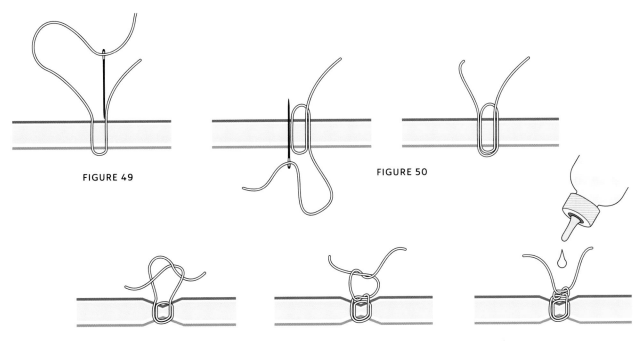

FIGURE 49

FIGURE 50

FIGURE 51

FIGURE 52

FIGURE 53

10" (25.4 cm)

FIGURE 54

¼" (6 mm)

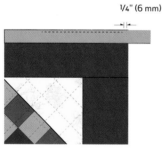

FIGURE 55

your chosen seam line. If you'll be left with more than ⅛" (3 mm) of batting/backing extending beyond any part of the quilt top edge after trimming, trim the top itself as much as necessary to bring the batting/backing extension to less than ⅛" (3 mm).

Trim the corner first, using the ruler to ensure a right angle, then move the ruler down the length of the quilt. Align the ruler with the chosen seam line and overlap the previously cut edge so you are trimming in a straight line. As you get to the bottom, do the same thing with the square end of the ruler as you did at the top, making another perfect right angle corner. Continue in this manner all around the quilt.

When you're done, check to see if any basting was trimmed and resew those areas. The three layers should be sewn together so they will act like one piece of fabric as you sew on the binding.

MAKING AND ATTACHING THE BINDING

Quilts can be bound with binding cut on the straight grain or on the bias. Bias binding is needed if a quilt has scalloped edges or rounded corners. All of the quilts in this book have been bound with straight-grain binding made from 2¼" (5.7 cm) wide strips sewn end-to-end with diagonal seams (**FIGURE 52**). Once you've sewn the strips together, fold the binding strip in half lengthwise, wrong sides together and raw edges aligned, and press (**FIGURE 53**).

Square up the quilted quilt, then beginning in the center of the bottom edge, place the binding strip against the right side of the quilt top. Align the binding strip raw edges with the quilt top raw edge, leaving a

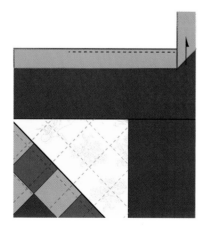

FIGURE 56

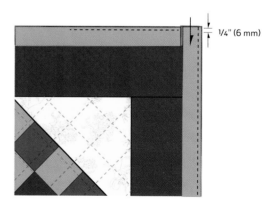

¼" (6 mm)

FIGURE 57

10" (25.4 cm) tail (**FIGURE 54**). Sew the binding to the quilt using a ¼" (6 mm) seam allowance. To miter the corners of your binding strip, stop stitching ¼" (6 mm) from the raw edge at the first corner and backstitch (**FIGURE 55**). Cut the thread and rotate the quilt 90°. At the corner, fold the binding strip back over itself to form a 45° fold (**FIGURE 56**). Holding the 45° angle with your left hand, fold the binding forward over itself forming a fold parallel to the edge of the quilt. Aligning the new fold with the raw edge, begin stitching again at the corner (**FIGURE 57**). Continue around the quilt in the same manner until you are 10–20" (25.4–50.8 cm) from where you began stitching, and backstitch.

Remove the quilt from under the presser foot and place it on a flat surface. Lay the first binding tail in place on the quilt top, aligning the raw edges. Repeat with the second binding tail. Crease the second binding tail where it meets the first tail's straight cut end. From the crease, measure the distance of the binding strip's cut width. For example, if the binding strips were cut 2¼" (5.7 cm) wide, the measurement would be 2¼" (5.7 cm). Cut the second tail straight across at that measurement. Open the tails. With right sides together, place one on top of the other at a right angle. Join the strips with a diagonal seam (**FIGURE 58**). (Before trimming, refold the strips to be sure they're not twisted.) Trim the seam allowance to ¼" (6 mm) and finger press open. Fold the binding strip in half lengthwise, as it was previously. It should lie perfectly flat. Continue sewing the binding strip to the starting point. Backstitch to secure, then turn the binding over the edge of the quilt and slipstitch in place (**FIGURE 59**).

SIGNING OR LABELING YOUR QUILT

It's important to either sign or label your quilt. You should include the name of the quiltmaker and quilter, the name of the quilt, and the city, state, date, and quilt pattern. A note about your thoughts, feelings, the recipient's name and occasion, if the quilt is a gift, can also be included.

My favorite way to make a label is to start with a piece of muslin ½" (1.3 cm) larger than my desired label and a piece of freezer paper the size of the finished label. On the dull side of the freezer paper, draw lines ¼" (6 mm) apart to act as a guide for writing on the label. Then, centering the freezer paper on the

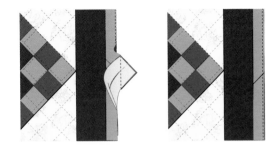

FIGURE 58

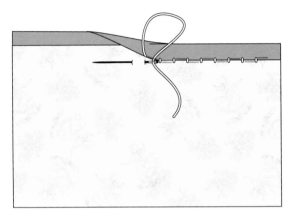

FIGURE 59

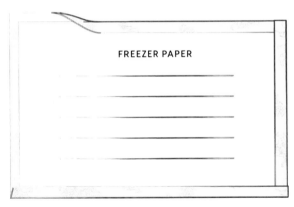

FREEZER PAPER

FIGURE 60

wrong side of the muslin, press the freezer paper to the muslin, and press the ¼" (6 mm) seam allowance over the edge of the freezer paper, forming a hem (**FIGURE 60**). Turn the muslin over and using the lines as a guide, write the information you want on your label with a permanent pen, such as a Pigma pen. Press with a dry iron. Remove the freezer paper from the back and pin the label in place on the quilt. Use a slipstitch to sew it to the quilt.

Chapter 2

QUILTS
AND
PROJECTS

The Ingalls family was familiar with cold weather. Fortunately, they could wrap themselves in the warm embrace of quilts. Pieced and quilted with diligence, made of fabric purchased with hard work, these quilts were meant to be used for many years. Of course, Laura, Mary, Ma, Carrie, and Grace appreciated more than the warmth and beauty their quilts provided. Quilting was one of the ways pioneer women could express their own personalities. In choosing fabrics, creating and selecting patterns, and quilting their own designs, pioneer quilters added fun and satisfaction to their lives. We love quilting for the same reasons today. As Laura said, "I'm beginning to learn that it is the sweet, simple things of life which are the real ones after all."

In this chapter, you'll find ten bed quilts as well as four smaller projects, which are perfect for giving or keeping.

WALNUT GROVE SAMPLER

Women in the 1850s through 1870s (the period covered by the *Little House* books) all learned how to sew, and many of them learned by making a quilt. Because they're easily pieced, the blocks in this quilt—the Churn Dash, Pinwheel, Snowball, Friendship Star, Sawtooth Star, Shadowbox, and Ohio Star—were among the most popular for young girls to try.

MATERIALS

5¼ yards (4.8 m) assorted medium (red, brown, and gray) prints and stripes

2¼ yards (2.1 m) assorted light (beige, cream, and tan) prints

3⅜ yards (3.1 m) large beige print for setting squares

8 yards (7.3 m) backing fabric

⅞ yard (0.8 m) complementary tan stripe fabric for binding

87" × 99" (221 cm × 251.5 cm) batting

Finished size: 78½" × 90½" (199.4cm × 229.9cm)
Pieced by Sherri Driver
Quilted by Donna Smith

CUTTING INSTRUCTIONS

Cut patches in the order listed. Each block is made from matching sets of patches. As you cut, put the patches in piles according to their blocks. When you're ready to sew a block, bring only the patches you'll need for that block to your machine. For example, when sewing a Churn Dash block, you will need 1 set of background patches and 1 set of shape patches.

To vary the design, play with the stripes and directional prints. You can purchase extra of those fabrics and experiment with different cutting ideas. (For tips, see Fussy-Cutting in Chapter 1).

FROM ASSORTED MEDIUM PRINTS AND STRIPES, CUT:

For Pinwheel blocks, cut:
26 pairs of matching 3⅞" (9.8 cm) squares

For Snowball blocks, cut:
(22) 6½" (16.5 cm) squares for centers
22 sets of 4 matching 2½" (6.4 cm) squares for corners

For Shadowbox blocks, cut:
(6) 2⅝" (6.7 cm) squares for Shadowbox centers
6 pairs of matching 2⅜" (6 cm) squares; cut in half diagonally, for inner Shadowbox rings
6 pairs of matching 3" (7.6 cm) squares; cut in half diagonally, for middle Shadowbox rings
6 pairs of matching 3⅞" (9.8 cm) squares; cut in half diagonally, for outer Shadowbox rings

For Friendship Star blocks, cut 9 matched sets (3 patches each) of:
(2) 2⅞" (7.3 cm) squares
(1) 2½" (6.4 cm) square

For Friendship Star backgrounds, cut 9 matched sets (6 patches each) of:
(2) 2⅞" (7.3 cm) squares
(4) 2½" (6.4 cm) squares

For Churn Dash blocks, cut 14 matched sets (7 patches each) of:
(2) 2⅞" (7.3 cm) squares
(4) 1½" × 2½" (3.8 cm × 6.4 cm) rectangles
(1) 2½" (6.4 cm) square

For Churn Dash backgrounds, cut 14 matched sets (6 patches each) of:
(2) 2⅞" (7.3 cm) squares
(4) 1½" × 2½" (3.8 cm × 6.4 cm) rectangles

For Sawtooth Star blocks, cut 5 matched sets (9 patches each) of:
(8) 2" (5.1 cm) squares
(1) 3½" (8.9 cm) square

For Sawtooth Star backgrounds, cut 5 matched sets (8 patches each) of:
(4) 2" × 3½" (5.1 cm × 8.9 cm) rectangles
(4) 2" (5.1 cm) squares

For Ohio Star blocks, cut 2 matched sets (3 patches each) of:
(2) 3¼" (8.3 cm) squares
(1) 2½" (6.4 cm) square

FROM ASSORTED LIGHT PRINTS, CUT:

For Pinwheel blocks, cut:
26 pairs of matching 3⅞" (9.8 cm) squares

For Sawtooth Star blocks, cut 5 matched sets (9 patches each) of:
(8) 2" (5.1 cm) squares
(1) 3½" (8.9 cm) square

For Sawtooth Star backgrounds, cut 5 matched sets (8 patches each) of:
(4) 2" × 3½" (5.1 cm × 8.9 cm) rectangles
(4) 2" (5.1 cm) squares

For Friendship Star blocks, cut 9 matched sets (3 patches each) of:
(2) 2⅞" (7.3 cm) squares
(1) 2½" (6.4 cm) square

For Friendship Star backgrounds, cut 9 matched sets (6 patches each) of:
(2) 2⅞" (7.3 cm) squares
(4) 2½" (6.4 cm) squares

For Ohio Star backgrounds, cut 2 matched sets (6 patches each) of:
(2) 3¼" (8.3 cm) squares
(4) 2½" (6.4 cm) squares

FROM LARGE BEIGE PRINT, CUT:
(97) 6½" (16.5 cm) squares for setting squares

FROM BINDING FABRIC, CUT:
(10) 2¼" (5.7 cm) × WOF (width-of-fabric) strips

HALF-PINT TIP
Cutting Fabric

Because of the way fabric is woven, it has three grains. The *lengthwise grain* runs parallel to the selvages (the uncut edges of the fabric) and stretches very little, if at all. The *crosswise grain* runs perpendicular to the selvages and stretches enough to be noticeable when you pull on the fabric. The *bias grain* runs on the diagonal and stretches more than either of the others.

It's important to cut strips and patches on the correct grain, so they fit together well and don't stretch out of shape. When cutting most patches, such as squares and rectangles, make sure the straight edges of the patch aren't cut on the bias grain of the fabric. The straight edges should be cut parallel or perpendicular to the selvages. It's a good idea to cut large borders on the lengthwise grain, if possible, so they are stable. Take advantage of the bias grain's stretchiness by using it when you are sewing curves or need a gracefully meandering stem. When cutting, be sure to follow instructions that specify grain.

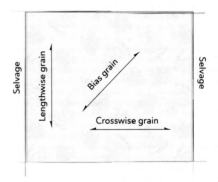

PIECING THE BLOCKS

FINISHED BLOCK SIZES: 6" (15.2 CM) SQUARE

PINWHEEL BLOCKS

1. Referring to **FIGURE 1**, draw a diagonal line on the wrong side of a light 3⅞" (9.8 cm) square. Place the square on a medium 3⅞" (9.8 cm) square, right sides together and edges aligned. Sew a ¼" (6 mm) seam on each side of the marked line. Cut the squares along the marked line, then open each side and press to make 2 pieced squares. Use the same fabrics to make 2 more matching pieced squares. Make 26 sets of 4 matching pieced squares.

2. Sew 1 set of 4 matching pieced squares together, orienting them as shown (**FIGURE 2**) to make 1 Pinwheel block. Make 26 blocks.

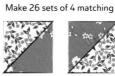

Make 26 sets of 4 matching

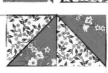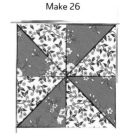

Make 26

FIGURE 1

FIGURE 2

Pinwheel Block

SNOWBALL BLOCKS

3. Draw a diagonal line on the wrong side of 4 matching 2½" (6.4 cm) medium squares. Referring to **FIGURE 3**, place 1 marked square on the corner of (1) contrasting 6½" (16.5 cm) medium square, right sides

together and edges aligned. Stitch on the drawn line. Trim excess fabric (**FIGURE 4**), then flip the new corner open and press. Repeat on the 3 remaining corners to make 1 Snowball block. Make 22 blocks.

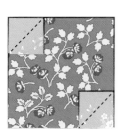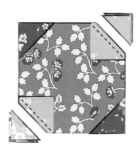

Make 22

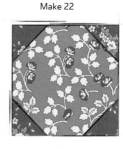

FIGURE 3

FIGURE 4

Snowball Block

FRIENDSHIP STAR BLOCKS

4. Combine matching sets of Friendship Star block patches in a light fabric with matching sets of Friendship Star block background patches in a medium fabric, and vice versa. Using the technique in step 1 of the Pinwheel blocks to make pieced squares, sew together 36 pairs of light and medium 2⅞" (7.3 cm) squares to make 18 total sets of 4 matching pieced squares each (**FIGURE 5**).

5. Referring to **FIGURE 6**, for each block arrange 3 rows with 1 set of 4 matching pieced squares, the matching set of 4 light-colored 2½" (6.4 cm) squares, and the matching medium-colored 2½" (6.4 cm) square. Stitch the rows together as shown to make 1 Friendship Star block. Make 18 blocks.

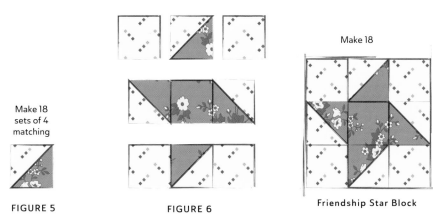

Make 18 sets of 4 matching

FIGURE 5

FIGURE 6

Make 18

Friendship Star Block

CHURN DASH BLOCKS

When making pieced squares in steps 6 and 7, keep in mind that only 2 fabrics are used in each block.

6. Using the technique in step 1, sew together 28 pairs of contrasting 2⅞" (7.3 cm) squares to make 14 total sets of 4 matching pieced triangle squares each (**FIGURE 7**).

7. Referring to **FIGURE 8**, join 2 contrasting 1½" × 2½" (3.8 cm × 6.4 cm) rectangles together to make a pieced rectangle square. Make 4 matching sets.

8. Referring to **FIGURE 9**, arrange 3 rows of 4 matching pieced triangle squares, 4 matching pieced rectangle squares, and a coordinating 2½" (6.5cm) square for the center. Sew the rows together to make 1 Churn Dash block. Make 14 blocks.

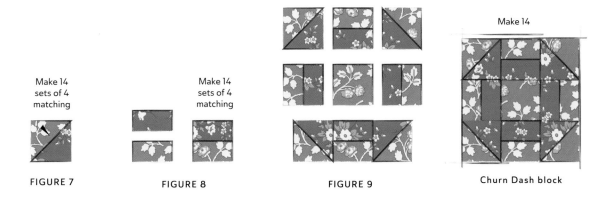

Make 14 sets of 4 matching

FIGURE 7

Make 14 sets of 4 matching

FIGURE 8

FIGURE 9

Make 14

Churn Dash block

SAWTOOTH STAR BLOCKS

9. Draw a diagonal line on the wrong side of 8 matching light or medium 2" (5.1 cm) squares. Referring to **FIGURE 10**, place 1 marked square on a contrasting 2" × 3½" (5.1 cm × 8.9 cm) rectangle, right sides together and edges aligned. Sew on the marked line, then trim the excess fabric, open the pieces, and press. Using a matching 2" (5.1 cm) square, repeat on the opposite end of the rectangle to make a pieced rectangle. Make 10 total sets of 4 matching pieced rectangles.

10. Referring to **FIGURE 11**, arrange 3 rows using 1 set of 4 matching pieced rectangles, the matching set of 4 light or medium 2" (5.1 cm) squares, and a coordinating light or medium 3½" (8.9 cm) square. Stitch the rows together to make 1 Sawtooth Star block. Make 10 blocks.

Make 10 sets of 4 matching

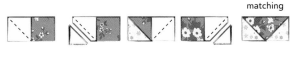

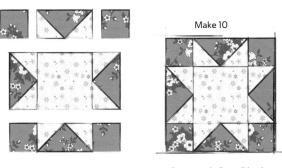

FIGURE 10

Make 10

FIGURE 11

Sawtooth Star Block

SHADOWBOX BLOCKS

11. Referring to **FIGURE 12**, sew 1 set of 4 matching 2⅜" (6 cm) triangles to a contrasting 2⅝" (6.7 cm) square as shown. In the same manner, add 1 set of 4 matching 3" (7.6 cm) triangles to complete the block center (**FIGURE 13**).

12. Sew 1 set of 4 matching 3⅞" (9.8 cm) triangles to the block center to complete 1 Shadowbox block (**FIGURE 14**). Make 6 blocks.

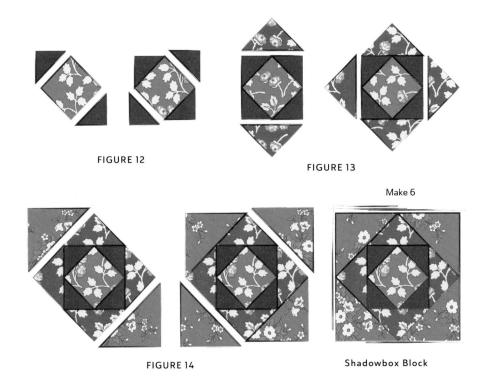

FIGURE 12

FIGURE 13

Make 6

FIGURE 14

Shadowbox Block

OHIO STAR BLOCKS

13. Draw 2 diagonal lines on the wrong sides of 2 matching light 3¼" (8.3 cm) squares. Referring to **FIGURE 15**, place 1 marked square on a contrasting 3¼" (8.3 cm) square, right sides together and aligning the edges. Sew a ¼" (6 mm) seam on each side of one of the lines. Cut on the unsewn line first, then on the remaining drawn line. Open and press each quarter to make 4 matching pieced triangles (2 of each orientation). Repeat to make a total of 8 matching pieced triangles (4 of each orientation). Using the remaining 3¼" (8.3 cm) squares, make a second set of 8 matching pieced triangles.

14. Sew 2 matching triangles together to make a pieced square (**FIGURE 16**). Make 2 sets of 4 matching pieced squares.

15. Referring to **FIGURE 17**, arrange 3 rows using 1 set of 4 matching pieced squares, 1 matching set of (4) 2½" (6.5 cm) squares, and a matching 2½" (6.4 cm) square. Stitch the rows together to make 1 Ohio Star Block. Make 2 blocks.

Make 2 sets of 8 matching

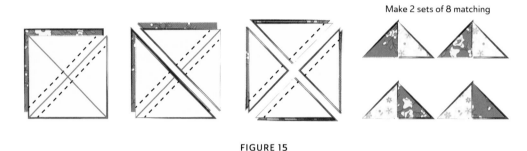

FIGURE 15

Make 2 sets
of 4 matching

FIGURE 16

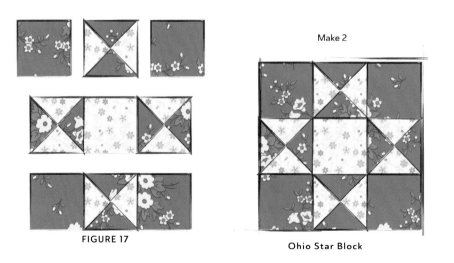

FIGURE 17

Make 2

Ohio Star Block

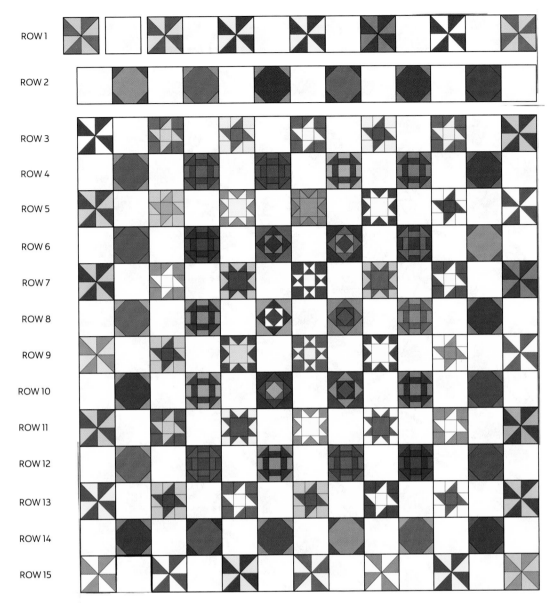

ROW 1
ROW 2
ROW 3
ROW 4
ROW 5
ROW 6
ROW 7
ROW 8
ROW 9
ROW 10
ROW 11
ROW 12
ROW 13
ROW 14
ROW 15

ASSEMBLY DIAGRAM

ASSEMBLING THE QUILT TOP

16. The blocks in the quilt are arranged so they form concentric rings by block type with the two Ohio Star blocks in the center. For ease of sewing, the blocks are sewn together in horizontal rows. Referring to the quilt photo and the **Assembly Diagram**, lay out the blocks and 6½" (16.5 cm) setting squares in concentric rings on a design wall or other large, flat surface.

17. Removing 1 row of blocks at a time, sew 15 rows of 13 blocks each, numbering each row as you replace it on the design wall. Stitch the rows together, matching adjacent seams, to complete the quilt top.

FINISHING

18. Piece the quilt backing lengthwise, making it at least 8" (20.3 cm) longer and wider than the quilt top. Layer the backing (wrong-side up), the batting, and the quilt top (right-side up) and baste them together.

19. Quilt as desired, then bind (see Making and Attaching the Binding in Chapter 1). The setting squares feature feathered wreaths, while every block type has a different quilted design. For example, the Pinwheel blocks have plumes quilted in each triangle, the Shadowbox blocks have a posy centered in each, and the Sawtooth Star blocks are filled with petaled flowers.

MY PEACE
OF THE PRAIRIE

I fell in love with two of the fabrics in this quilt when I was sewing the checkerboard areas, so I decided to use them again in the outer border and binding. The outer border features my favorite little blue-on-blue floral and the binding is a cheerful green floral with little yellow, white, and blue flowers that was also used in the quilt center. If you want to use a fabric in multiple parts of a quilt, remember to buy enough yardage for all the chosen areas.

MATERIALS

4¼ yards (3.9 m) cream and blue print for the background and inner borders

½ yard (0.5 m) each of 4 assorted green florals/textures for the quilt center

⅜ yard (0.3 m) each of 3 assorted blue florals/textures for the pieced border

½ yard (0.5 m) medium blue floral for the outer border

5½ yards (5 m) backing fabric

¾ yard (0.7 m) for binding

79" × 96" (200.7 cm × 243.8 cm) batting

Finished size: 70⅜" × 87⅜" (178.8 cm × 221.9 cm)
Pieced by Laura Stone Roberts
Quilted by Karen Dovala

CUTTING INSTRUCTIONS

For the best use of fabric, cut the strips and patches below in the order listed.

From the cream and blue print, cut:

(2) 6⅛" × 62¾" (15.6 cm × 159.4 cm) strips, cut on the lengthwise grain

(2) 6⅛" × 57⅛" (15.6 cm x 145.1 cm) strips, cut on the lengthwise grain

(10) 4½" (11.4 cm) × WOF (width-of-fabric) strips

(6) 2½" (6.4 cm) × WOF strips

(7) 7" (17.8 cm) squares; cut each in half twice diagonally to make 28 quarter-square triangles

(50) 4⅛" (10.5 cm) squares; cut each in half twice diagonally to make 200 quarter-square triangles

(2) 3¾" (9.5 cm) squares; cut each in half diagonally to make 4 half-square triangles

From the assorted green florals/textures, cut a total of:

(10) 4½" (11.4 cm) × WOF strips

(12) 4½" (11.4 cm) squares

From the assorted blue florals/textures, cut:

(12) 2½" (6.4 cm) × WOF strips

(4) 4⅛" (10.5 cm) squares; cut each in half twice diagonally to make 16 quarter-square triangles

(8) 2½" (6.4 cm) squares

From the medium blue floral, cut a total of:

(2) 1½" × 85⅜" (3.8 cm × 216.9 cm) strips, pieced from 5 WOF strips

(2) 1½" × 70⅜" (3.8 cm × 178.8 cm) strips, pieced from 4 WOF strips

From the binding fabric, cut:

(9) 2¼" (5.7 cm) × WOF strips

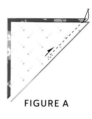 

PIECING THE QUILT CENTER

1. Referring to **FIGURE 1**, join (1) 4½" (11.4 cm) × WOF cream and blue strip to (1) 4½" (11.4 cm) × WOF assorted green strip to make a strip set. Make 10 strip sets total. Cut the strip sets into a total of (76) 4½" (11.4 cm) wide segments.

2. Sew 2 different segments together to make a Four-Patch block (**FIGURE 2**). Make 38 Four-Patch blocks.

3. Sew (2) 7" (17.8 cm) cream and blue quarter-square triangles to adjoining sides of (1) 4½" (11.4 cm) assorted green square as shown to make a setting triangle (**FIGURE 3**). Make 8.

4. Referring to **FIGURE 4**, sew (2) 7" (17.8 cm) cream and blue quarter-square triangles to opposite sides of (1) 4½" (11.4 cm) assorted green square. Add (1) 3¾" (9.5 cm) cream and blue half-square triangle as shown to make a corner triangle. Make 4.

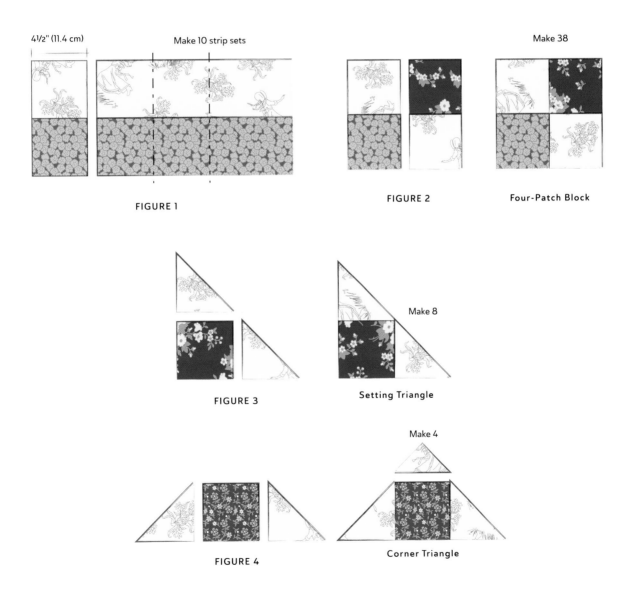

4½" (11.4 cm)　　　Make 10 strip sets　　　Make 38

FIGURE 1

FIGURE 2　　　Four-Patch Block

Make 8

FIGURE 3　　　Setting Triangle

Make 4

FIGURE 4　　　Corner Triangle

7" (17.8 cm)

7" (17.8 cm)

FIGURE 5

FIGURE 6

¼" (6 mm)

FIGURE 7

5. Referring to **FIGURE 5** and noting the orientation of the Four-Patches, sew together a setting triangle, 2 Four-Patches, and (1) 7" (17.8 cm) cream and blue quarter-square triangle (positioned as shown) to make the first diagonal row of the quilt center. In a similar manner, make the 7 remaining diagonal rows as shown, using setting triangles, Four-Patches, and the 3 remaining 7" (17.8 cm) cream and blue quarter-square triangles.

6. Aligning the seams, sew the rows together to make the quilt center (**FIGURE 6**). Add the corner triangles as shown. Notice 3 cream and blue squares extend beyond both the top and bottom edges. Trim the squares even, ¼" (6 mm) beyond the outer corners of the assorted green squares (**FIGURE 7**).

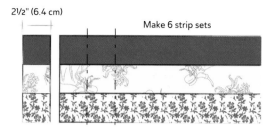

2½" (6.4 cm)

Make 6 strip sets

FIGURE 8

PIECING THE BORDER STRIPS

7. Referring to **FIGURE 8**, sew together (1) 2½" (6.4 cm) × WOF cream and blue strip and (2) 2½" (6.4 cm) × WOF assorted blue strips to make a strip set. Make 6 strip sets. Cut the strip sets into (92) 2½" (6.4 cm) wide segments.

8. Referring to **FIGURE 9** and noting the orientation of the triangles, sew (2) 4⅛" (10.5 cm) cream and blue quarter-square triangles to the ends of 1 segment to make a border unit. Make 92 border units.

9. Referring to **FIGURE 10,** make a border end unit by sewing together (1) 4⅛" (10.5 cm) assorted blue triangle, a 2½" (6.4 cm) cream and blue square, a 2½" (6.4 cm) assorted blue square, and a 4⅛" (10.5 cm) cream and blue triangle. Make 8 border end units.

10. Sew together (1) 4⅛" (10.5 cm) assorted blue triangle and (1) 4⅛" (10.5 cm) cream and blue triangle in the orientation shown to make a border corner (**FIGURE 11**). Make 8 border corners.

11. Referring to **FIGURE 12** and aligning seams, sew together 24 border units, 2 border end units, and 2 border corners to make a side border strip. Make 2 side border strips. In the same manner and referring to **FIGURE 13**, sew together 22 border units, 2 border end units, and 2 border corners to make a top/bottom border strip. Make 2 border strips.

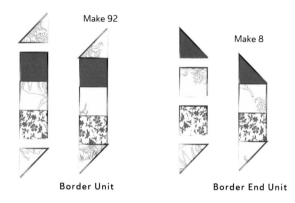

Make 92

Border Unit

FIGURE 9

Make 8

Border End Unit

FIGURE 10

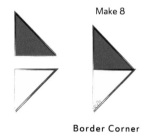

Make 8

Border Corner

FIGURE 11

Make 2 side border strips

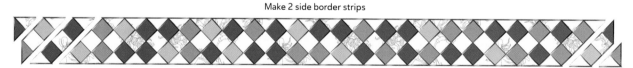

FIGURE 12

Make 2 top/bottom border strips

FIGURE 13

ASSEMBLY DIAGRAM

ASSEMBLING THE QUILT TOP

Refer to the **Assembly Diagram** throughout assembly.

12. Stitch the 62¾" (159.3 cm) cream and blue strips to the sides of the quilt center. Sew the 57⅛" (145 cm) cream and blue strips to the top and bottom. Sew 1 pieced side border strip to each side. Stitch 1 pieced top/bottom border strip to the top and the other to the bottom.

13. Sew the medium blue 85⅜" (216.8 cm) strips to the sides. Sew the medium blue 70⅜" (178.7 cm) strips to the top and bottom to complete the quilt top.

FINISHING

14. Piece the quilt backing lengthwise (it should be at least 8" (20.3 cm) longer and wider than the quilt top). Layer the backing (wrong-side up), the batting, and the quilt top (right-side up) and baste them together.

15. Quilt as desired, then bind the quilt with the binding fabric strips (see Making and Attaching the Binding in Chapter 1). Note: The featured quilt was machine quilted in an allover posy-and-swirl design, using cream thread.

A JOLLY DOLLY AFTERNOON

On rare occasions as a child, I would read something in a book that would become like a memory of my very own. The Christmas when Laura gets a rag doll in *Little House in the Big Woods* is one of those special memories. I can picture her doll, Charlotte, perfectly, as well as the astonished look on Laura's face when she first sees her. I can imagine the quiet joy she must have felt as she fell asleep on Christmas night holding Charlotte.

The dolls in this quilt each wear a dress, a tie (belt), and a pair of shoes. Every 10" (25.4 cm) floral square provides two dresses and a minimum of two ties and four shoes. Have fun dressing your dolls any way you wish. Maybe you'll have a couple of dolls with matching outfits. Or a doll with mismatched shoes. And the same goes for the faces. You may wish to draw the facial features in the same colors, or perhaps you will mix it up and give your dollies blue or brown eyes and a red or pink mouth. It's entirely up to you.

MATERIALS

6½ yards (5.9 m) tan print for the block back-grounds, sashing, setting triangles, and inner border

1¾ yards (1.6 m) light yellow/pink floral print for the cornerstones and outer border

1¼ yards (1.1 m) green flower print for the sashing squares and binding

10" (25.4 cm) square each of 9 assorted light and medium floral prints and textures for the dresses, ties, and shoes

½ yard (0.5 m) assorted yellow/gold, brown, black, and red textures, mottles, and prints for the hair

⅞ yard (0.8 m) assorted skin-toned solids and mottles for the arms, legs, and faces

6 yards (5.5 m) backing fabric

80" × 98" (203.2 cm × 248.9 cm) batting

Pigma pens (size 05), in colors for the dolls' eyes and mouths

3½ yards (3.2 m) of paper-backed fusible web (at least 17" [43.2 cm] wide) for the appliqué

Doll templates (see Chapter 3)

Finished size: 72" × 89¾" (182.9 cm × 228 cm)
Pieced and appliquéd by Kathy Lewis
Quilted by Karen Dovala

CUTTING INSTRUCTIONS

The templates for the dolls and their clothes are printed reversed and without turn-under allowances for use with paper-backed fusible web. If you wish to hand-appliqué the dolls, add turn-under allowances.

For the best use of fabric, cut the strips and patches below in the order listed. **Note:** Border strips include extra length for trimming.

From the tan print, cut:
(2) 3" × 79" (7.6 cm × 200.7 cm) strips, cut on the lengthwise grain for the inner border
(2) 3" × 66" (7.6 cm × 167.6 cm) strips, cut on the lengthwise grain for the inner border
(14) 1⅜" (3.5 cm) × WOF (width-of-fabric) strips
(3) 20" (50.8 cm) squares; cut in half twice diagonally to make 12 quarter-square setting triangles (you will have 2 extra)
(2) 13" (33 cm) squares; cut in half diagonally to make 4 half-square corner triangles
(18) 12½" (31.8 cm) squares
(72) 3¾" (9.5 cm) squares; cut in half twice diagonally to make 288 quarter-square triangles
(158) 2⅛" (5.4 cm) squares; cut in half diagonally to make 316 half-square triangles

From the yellow/pink floral, cut:
(2) 5½" × 84" (14 cm × 213.4 cm) strips, pieced together from 5 WOF strips for the outer border
(2) 5½" × 76" (14 cm × 193 cm) strips, pieced together from 4 WOF strips for the outer border
(31) 2¼" (5.7 cm) squares for the cornerstones

From the green flower print, cut:
(14) 1⅜" (3.5 cm) × WOF strips
(9) 2¼" (5.7 cm) × WOF strips for the binding

From each of the 9 assorted floral prints, cut:
1 each of Templates F and Fr (F reversed)
1 each of Templates G and Gr (G reversed)
1 each of Templates H and Hr (H reversed)
1 each of Templates I and Ir (I reversed)

From the yellow/gold, brown, black, and red textures, mottles, and prints, cut a total of:
9 each of Templates A and Ar (A reversed)
9 each Templates K and Kr (K reversed)

From the assorted skin-toned solids and mottles, cut a total of:
9 each Templates B and Br (B reversed)
9 each Templates C and Cr (C reversed)
9 each Templates D and Dr (D reversed)
9 each Templates E and Er (E reversed)
9 each Templates J and Jr (J reversed)

HALF-PINT TIP
Make Practice Blocks

It never hurts to make a practice block, especially if you're learning a technique. Keep all of your practice blocks and make a one-of-a-kind sampler quilt just for yourself.

APPLIQUÉING THE DOLLY BLOCKS
Finished size: 10" (25.4 cm) square

Follow the manufacturer's instructions for using the paper-backed fusible web. **Note:** The 12½" (31.8 cm) tan background squares are cut oversized to allow for shrinkage during appliqué.

1. Trace templates A/Ar-K/Kr on the paper side of the fusible web. Cut the templates apart, leaving a small margin beyond the drawn lines. Fuse the templates to the wrong side of the appropriate fabrics and cut them out on the drawn lines.

2. Finger press a 12½" (31.8 cm) tan square in half on both diagonals. Referring to **FIGURE 1** and using the fold lines as a placement guide, position templates A-K in alphabetical order on the square, keeping in mind that the square will be trimmed to 10½" (26.7 cm). Fuse the templates in place, then trace the face onto the dolly with the Pigma pen or other pens. Make 9 Dolly blocks.

3. In the same manner as step 2, use templates Ar-Kr to make 9 Reversed Dolly blocks (**FIGURE 2**).

4. Edgestitch the appliqué using a machine straight or decorative stitch, in either matching thread or monofilament (see Edgestitching Appliqué in Chapter 1). Centering the appliqué, trim the blocks to 10½" (26.7 cm) square.

PIECING SASHING STRIPS AND CORNERSTONES

It's important to have an accurate ¼" (6 mm) seam allowance when piecing the sashing strips. You may wish to sew a test strip before piecing the rest. **Note:** Use care when handling the bias edges of the triangles to prevent distortion.

5. Join 1 tan and 1 green 1⅜" (3.5 cm) wide strip to make a strip set. Press seam allowances toward the darker fabric. Make 14 strip sets. Cut the strip sets into (384) 1⅜" (3.5 cm) wide segments (**FIGURE 3**).

FIGURE 1

FIGURE 2

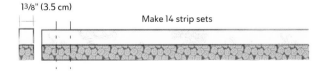

1⅜" (3.5 cm)

Make 14 strip sets

FIGURE 3

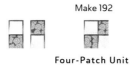

Make 192

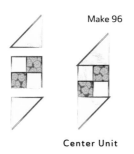

Four-Patch Unit

FIGURE 4

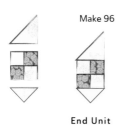

Make 96

End Unit

FIGURE 5

Make 96

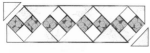

Center Unit

FIGURE 6

Make 48

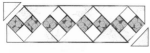

Sashing Strip

FIGURE 7

Make 31

Cornerstone

FIGURE 8

6. Sew 2 segments together to make 1 Four-Patch unit (**FIGURE 4**). Make 192 Four-Patch units.

7. Sew (1) 3¾" (9.5 cm) tan quarter-square triangle to one side of a Four-Patch unit as shown, then sew (1) 2⅛" (5.3 cm) tan print half-square triangle to the opposite side to complete a sashing strip end unit (**FIGURE 5**). Make 96 end units.

8. Sew (2) 3¾" (9.5 cm) tan quarter-square triangles to opposite sides of a Four-Patch unit as shown to make a sashing strip center unit (**FIGURE 6**). Make 96.

9. Referring to **FIGURE 7**, arrange 2 sashing strip end units and 2 center units as shown. Sew the units together. Add (2) 2⅛" (5.3 cm) tan half-square triangles to the remaining corners. Make 48 sashing strips.

10. Referring to **FIGURE 8**, finger press (1) 2¼" (5.7 cm) yellow square in half lengthwise and crosswise and (4) 2⅛" (5.3 cm) tan half-square triangles in half as shown. Aligning the folds, sew 2 of the triangles to opposite sides of the square. Join the remaining triangles to complete the square. Make 31 cornerstones.

ASSEMBLING THE QUILT TOP

Note: Setting triangles are cut oversized for trimming.

11. Referring to the **Assembly Diagram**, assemble the rows as follows:

Row 1: Sew 1 cornerstone to each end of a sashing strip. Noting the orientation, sew sashing strips to opposite sides of 1 Dolly block. Add the sashing strip with cornerstones to the top left side of the block. Add (2) 20" (50.8cm) tan quarter-square setting triangles.

Row 2: Join 4 cornerstones and 3 sashing strips, alternating, to make a cornerstone strip. Sew together 4 sashing strips and 3 Dolly blocks to make a block strip. Sew the cornerstone strip to the top left side of the block strip. Add (2) 20" (50.8cm) tan quarter-square setting triangles.

Row 3: Sew 6 cornerstones and 5 sashing strips together to make a cornerstone strip. Join 5 Dolly blocks and 6 sashing strips to make a block strip. Sew the cornerstone strip to the left side of the block strip, then add (1) 20" (50.8cm) tan quarter-square setting triangle to the left end of the row. Join 7 cornerstones

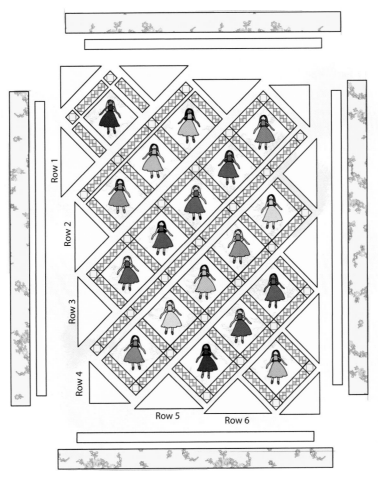

Assembly Diagram

and 6 sashing strips to make the center cornerstone strip, and then add it to the previous row.

Row 4: Sew together 5 Dolly blocks and 6 sashing strips to make a block row. Join 6 cornerstones and 5 sashing strips to make a cornerstone strip. Sew the cornerstone strip to the bottom right side of the block strip. Add a 20" (50.8cm) tan setting triangle to the right end of the row.

Rows 5 and 6: Continue in this manner to make the remaining 2 diagonal rows. Add the 4 tan 13" (33 cm) triangles to the corners. Trim all of the edges to ¼" (6 mm) beyond the cornerstone points, making sure the corners of the quilt center are square.

12. Measure the length of the quilt from edge to edge through the middle. Trim the 79" (200.7 cm) tan strips to this length and sew 1 to each side of the quilt. Measure the width of the quilt from edge to edge through the middle. Trim both 66" (167.6 cm) strips

to this length and sew 1 to the top and the other to the bottom of the quilt.

13. Measure the length of the quilt again and trim the 84" (213.4 cm) yellow strips to this length. Sew 1 strip to each side of the quilt. Measure the width of the quilt and trim the 76" (193 cm) yellow strips to this measurement. Sew 1 strip to the top and the other to the bottom of the quilt.

FINISHING
14. Piece the quilt backing, making sure it is at least 8" (20.3 cm) longer and wider than the quilt top. Layer the backing (wrong-side up), the batting, and the quilt top (right-side up) and baste them together.

15. Quilt as desired, then bind the quilt with the green flower print.

SINGING WILDFLOWERS

Goldenrod, clover, violets and buttercups, black-eyed Susans and wild roses…these are just some of the wildflowers mentioned in the *Little House* books. In *On the Banks of Plum Creek*, Laura and Mary walk to school on a dusty road past green prairie grass and fields of flowers. And in the same book, warm yellow sunshine pours over Laura's nightgown when she awakens in the family's new house and looks out through her own little sashed window. I like to think that this quilt captures those images of sweet flowers next to dusty roads, and warm sunshine blessing a little girl's flower-strewn world.

MATERIALS

5 1/2 yards (5 m) tan prairie print for the blocks and border

4 1/4 yards (3.9 m) total assorted small florals for the blocks

2 1/8 yards (1.9 m) yellow flower print for the diamonds and binding

9 3/8 yards (8.6 m) backing fabric

105" (266.7 cm) square batting

3 1/2 yards (3.2 m) paper-backed fusible web (at least 17" [43.2 cm] wide) for the appliqué

See-through template plastic

Diamond template (see Chapter 3)

Finished size: 96½" (245.1 cm) square
Pieced and appliquéd by Katie Melich, Rae Strauss, and Gwen Barlow
Quilted by Donna Smith

CUTTING INSTRUCTIONS

For the best use of fabric, cut the strips and patches in the order listed. **Note**: Border strips include extra length for trimming. The diamond template is printed without turn-under allowances to use with paper-backed fusible web. If you wish to hand-appliqué the diamonds, add turn-under allowances.

From the tan prairie print, cut:
(2) 6½" × 100" (16.5 cm × 254 cm) strips, cut on the lengthwise grain
(2) 6½" × 88" (16.5 cm × 223.5 cm) strips, cut on the lengthwise grain
(25) 9" (22.9 cm) squares
(48) 6⅞" (17.3 cm) squares; cut in half diagonally to make 96 half-square triangles

From the assorted small florals, cut a total of:
(24) 9" (23 cm) squares
(50) 6⅞" (17.5 cm) squares; cut in half diagonally to make 100 half-square triangles

From the yellow flower print, cut:
(10) 2¼" (5.7 cm) × WOF (width-of-fabric) strips for the binding
100 diamond shapes (see Cutting Diamonds)

HALF-PINT TIP
Cutting Diamonds

Trace the diamond template onto template plastic and cut out. Referring to the **Diamond Cutting Diagram**, draw parallel lines 2⅜" (6 cm) apart lengthwise on the paper side of the fusible web. Position the template so that 2 opposite sides are aligned with the drawn lines, then trace the remaining sides. Nest the template edges, continuing to align the base with the drawn line. Continue in this manner until you have drawn 100 diamond shapes. Following the manufacturer's instructions, fuse the fusible web to the wrong side of the yellow flower print, then cut the diamonds apart on the drawn lines.

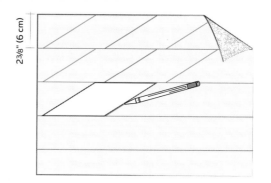

2⅜" (6 cm)

DIAMOND CUTTING DIAGRAM

MAKING THE BLOCKS
Finished size: 12" (30.5 cm) square

Note: When handling the bias edges of the triangles, use care to prevent distortion.

1. Finger press 2 matching triangles and a 9" (23 cm) tan square in half (**FIGURE 1**). Align the folds, then stitch the triangles to opposite sides of the square. In the same manner and referring to **FIGURE 2**, stitch another pair of matching triangles to the remaining sides of the square to complete the Wildflower block background (**FIGURE 3**). Trim the blocks to 12½" (31.8 cm) square. Make 25 total.

2. In the same manner, but using 4 tan triangles and (1) 9" (23 cm) assorted print square each, make 24 Broken Sash blocks (**FIGURE 4**).

3. Finger press a Wildflower block background in half lengthwise and widthwise (**FIGURE 5**). Referring to **FIGURE 6**, position a prepared diamond shape as shown, with one end at the exact center of the block and the opposite end ¼" (6 mm) from both edges at the block corner. Fuse in place. Repeat with 3 more diamonds to complete 1 Wildflower block (**FIGURE 7**). Make 25 blocks.

4. Edgestitch the diamonds using a machine decorative or straight stitch and matching thread (for tips, see Edgestitching Appliqué in Chapter 1).

FIGURE 1

FIGURE 2

Make 25

FIGURE 3

Make 24

Broken Sash Block

FIGURE 4

FIGURE 5

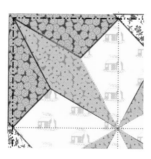

FIGURE 6

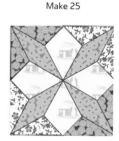

Make 25

Wildflower Block

FIGURE 7

ASSEMBLY DIAGRAM

ASSEMBLING THE QUILT TOP
Refer to the **Assembly Diagram** throughout.

5. Sew together 4 rows with 4 Wildflower blocks and 3 Broken Sash blocks each, alternating. Sew 3 rows of 4 Broken Sash blocks and 3 Wildflower blocks each, alternating.

6. Sew the rows together, alternating, to make the quilt center.

7. Measure the length of the quilt from edge to edge through the middle, then trim the 6½" × 88" (16.5 cm × 223.5 cm) tan strips to this length. Stitch 1 strip to each side of the quilt.

8. Measure the width of the quilt from edge to edge through the middle, then trim the 6½" × 100" (16.5 cm × 254 cm) tan strips to this measurement. Stitch 1 strip to the top and the other to the bottom of the quilt.

FINISHING
9. Piece the quilt backing, making sure it is at least 8" (20.3 cm) longer and wider than the quilt top. Layer the backing (wrong-side up), the batting, and the quilt top (right-side up) and baste them together.

10. Quilt as desired, then bind the quilt with the yellow flower print.

A SPRINGTIME OF SHIRTS

In *Little Town on the Prairie*, Laura spent six springtime weeks working from dawn to dusk sewing buttonholes and basting shirt facings to help earn money to send Mary to a college for the blind. The three shirt styles in this quilt are typical of the ones Laura worked on. When designing this quilt, I wanted to give it the feel of Mr. Clancy's dry goods store, so I used a narrow stripe as the background to offer the impression of a wallpaper interior behind the shirts. The fabric is also cut so that the stripes run vertically.

The instructions are written for fusible web appliqué. If you wish to hand-appliqué the shirts, add a ¼" (6 mm) turn-under allowance to each template. When appliquéing the collars, you'll be stacking the collar shapes on the neck facing shapes to give them extra dimension. The neck facings can be cut from 4" (10.2 cm) fabric scraps, so check your scrap basket before purchasing fabric for the facings.

MATERIALS

6⅜ yards (5.8 m) tan/gold/red narrow stripe with red flowers for the background and inner border

3 yards (2.7 m) brown/red wallpaper stripe for the outer border

⅜ yard (0.3 m) total assorted solids and textures for the neck facings

10" (25.4 cm) square each of 23 assorted prints and stripes for the shirts and collars

4¾ yards (4.3 m) paper-backed fusible web (at least 17" [43.2 cm] wide) for the appliqué

8¼ yards (7.5 m) backing fabric

¾ yard (0.7 m) small rust colored floral for binding

99" (251.5 cm) square batting

Appliqué pressing sheet *

Pigma pen (size 05), preferably brown or sepia

Shirt templates and tracing patterns (see Chapter 3)

*An appliqué pressing sheet is a nonstick, heatproof surface that lets you fuse appliqué pieces to one another before moving the prepared appliqué to its background square and fusing it in place there.

Finished size: 90½" (229.9 cm) square
Pieced and appliquéd by Martha Haynes
Quilted by Karen Dovala

CUTTING INSTRUCTIONS

For best use of fabric, cut the strips and patches below in the order they're listed. **Note:** The cutting instructions for the shirts, neck facings, and collars are on the templates in Chapter 3. The templates are printed reversed and without turn-under allowances for use with paper-backed fusible web. Each shirt and its collar shape is cut from (1) 10" (25.4 cm) square.

From the tan/gold/red narrow stripe with red flowers, cut:

(2) 3" × 75½" (7.6 cm × 191.8 cm) strips, pieced from 4 WOF (width-of-fabric) strips

(2) 3" × 70½" (7.6 cm × 179.1 cm) strips, cut on the lengthwise grain

(4) 5½" × 70½" (14 cm × 179.1 cm) strips, cut on the lengthwise grain

(23) 12½" (31.8 cm) squares for shirts

(4) 8" × 10½" (20.3 cm × 26.7 cm) rectangles, cut on the crosswise grain

(18) 5½" × 10½" (14 cm × 26.7 cm) rectangles, cut on the crosswise grain

From the brown/red wallpaper stripe, cut:

(4) 8" × 98" (20.3 cm × 248.9 cm) strips, cut on the lengthwise grain and centered on the floral stripe

From the rust colored floral, cut:

(10) 2¼" (5.7 cm) × WOF strips for binding

From the backing fabric, cut:

(2) 100" (254 cm) × WOF strips

(2) 20" × 50" (50.8 cm × 127 cm) strips

FIGURE 1

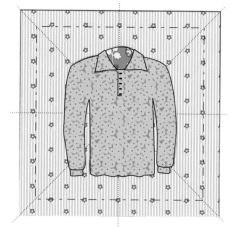

FIGURE 2

Make 8

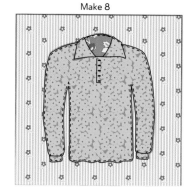

FIGURE 3

HALF-PINT TIP

Clip Corners Before Washing Fabric

Clip the corners of each piece of fabric before you wash it. Just a ¼" (6 mm) triangle cut from each corner will prevent long threads from tangling together in the wash, making big snarls and causing your fabrics to wrinkle badly.

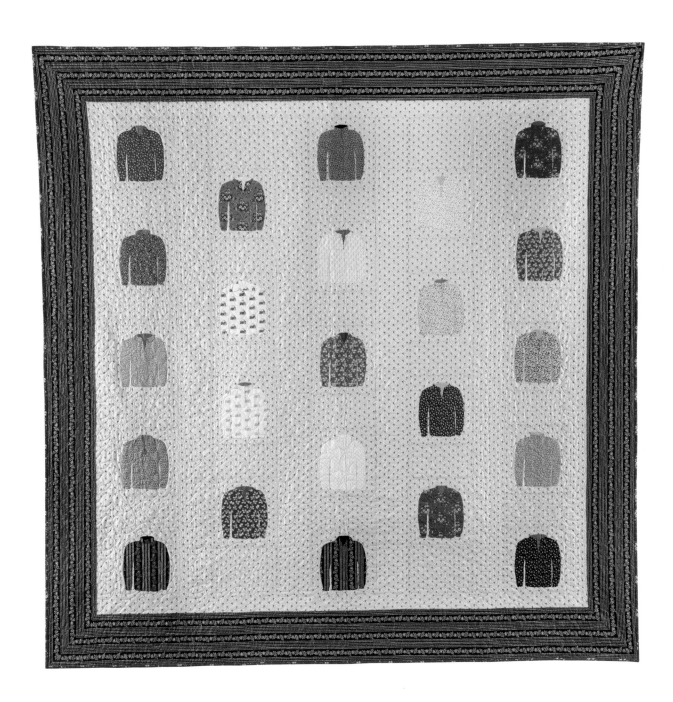

APPLIQUÉING THE SHIRT BLOCKS
Finished block size: 10" (25.4 cm) square

Follow the manufacturer's instructions for using the paper-backed fusible web. **Note:** The 12½" (31.8 cm) squares are cut oversized to allow for shrinkage during appliqué.

1. Trace the listed quantity of **Templates A-I** on the paper side of the fusible web. Cut the templates apart, leaving a small margin beyond the drawn lines, then fuse them to the wrong side of the appropriate fabrics. Cut out the shapes on the drawn lines.

2. Remove the paper from an A shape, its matching C and D shapes, and a coordinating B shape. Referring to **FIGURE 1**, position and layer the fabric shapes in alphabetical order on the appliqué pressing sheet, then fuse them together. Let the shirt cool, then remove it from the pressing sheet. Place the tracing guide for the farmer's shirt beneath the fused shapes, aligning the guide with the shirt as indicated. Using a Pigma pen, trace the lines and marks for the placket, buttons, and cuff seams onto the fused shirt. It may be helpful to use a light box when tracing. Or use repositionable tape to adhere the guide and shirt to a brightly lit window.

3. Referring to **FIGURE 2**, finger press a 12½" (31.8 cm) narrow stripe square in half lengthwise, widthwise, and on both diagonals. Using the folds as a guide, center the completed shirt on the square as shown with the stripes running vertically behind it. Fuse the shirt in place, then edgestitch the appliqué using matching thread and a machine blanket stitch or a machine straight stitch (see Edgestitching Appliqué in Chapter 1). If using a straight stitch, outline each shape with brown ink to make it stand out. Centering the appliqué, trim the square to 10½" (26.7 cm) square to complete 1 Farmer's Shirt block (**FIGURE 3**). Make 8 blocks.

4. In the same manner, use the remaining template shapes and 12½" (31.8 cm) squares to make 8 High-Necked Shirt blocks (**FIGURES 4 AND 5**) and 7 Laced Shirt blocks (**FIGURES 6 AND 7**). Use the tracing guide for garment details.

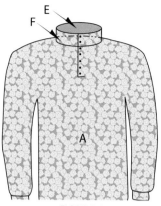

FIGURE 4

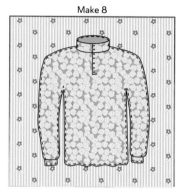

Make 8

High-Necked Shirt Block
FIGURE 5

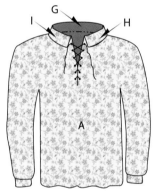

FIGURE 6

Make 7

Laced Shirt Block

FIGURE 7

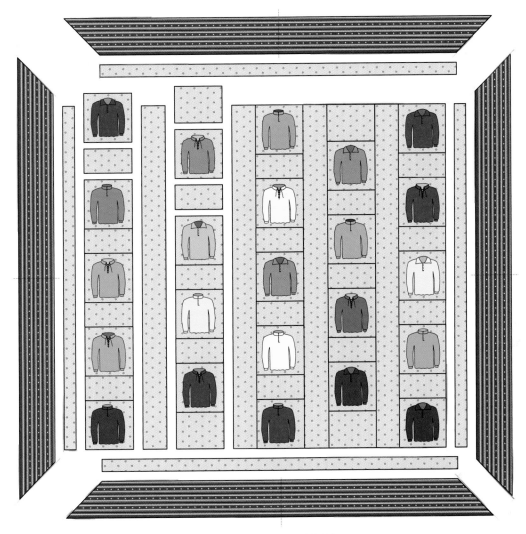

ASSEMBLY DIAGRAM

ASSEMBLING THE QUILT TOP
Refer to the **Assembly Diagram** throughout assembly.

5. Use a design wall or another large flat surface to arrange the shirt blocks. Sew 3 vertical rows with 5 shirt blocks and (4) 5½" × 10½" (14 cm × 26.7 cm) striped rectangles each. Sew 2 vertical rows with (2) 8" × 10½" (20.3 cm × 26.7 cm) striped rectangles, 4 shirt blocks, and (3) 5½" × 10½" (14 cm × 26.7 cm) striped rectangles each.

6. Stitch the rows and 5½" × 70½" (14 cm × 179.1 cm) striped strips together, alternating, as shown. Add the striped 70½" (179.1 cm) strips to the sides. Sew the striped 75½" (191.8 cm) strips to the top and bottom.

7. Finger press the 98" (248.9 cm) brown/red wallpaper stripe strips in half. Aligning the folds with the center of the middle block on each side and referring to Adding Mitered Borders in Chapter 1, add the border strips to all sides of the quilt. Sew and trim the mitered corners.

FINISHING
8. Sew the 50" (127 cm) backing fabric strips together end-to-end to make a pieced strip. Stitch a 98" (248.9 cm) strip to either side of the pieced strip and trim the edges even. Layer the backing (wrong-side up), the batting, and quilt top (right-side up), and baste them together.

9. Quilt as desired, then bind the quilt.

BIG SKY

I've been to places on the Great Plains where the night sky is almost overwhelming. The stars go right down to the ground, and it feels as if I'm falling up through the stars. I imagine that Laura Ingalls and her family experienced that sensation sometimes, along with an awareness of how immense and empty the land was in all directions. It would be comforting to know that you had a warm, safe house to retreat to when the world seemed too big.

MATERIALS

¼ yard (0.2 m) or fat quarter (18" × 21" [45.7 cm × 53.3 cm]) each of red/beige vine print, red/cream bouquet print, and yellow flower print for the house and stars

8" (20.3 cm) square red/brown stripe for the house

½ yard (0.5 m) tan/green prairie print for the house block

3" × 4" (7.6 cm × 10.2 cm) rectangle gray floral for the door and chimney

3⅛ yards (2.9 m) total of assorted pink, gold, green, blue, purple, and yellow florals and textures for the stars

7 ¼ yards (6.6 m) tan solid for the star backgrounds, quilt center, setting squares, and binding

8⅝ yards (7.9 m) backing fabric

94" (238.8 m) square batting

Finished size: 85½" (217.2 cm) square
Pieced by Laurie Bevan
Quilted by Donna Smith

CUTTING INSTRUCTIONS

For the best use of fabric, cut strips and patches in the order listed. The striped patches are cut so that the stripes are horizontal in the house block to resemble logs. The florals and textures in the stars are placed randomly for a playful feel. For monochromatic stars, cut additional pieces accordingly.

From the red/beige vine print, cut:

For the stars:

(1) 3" (7.6 cm) square

(1) 2½" (6.4 cm) square

(10) 2" (5.1 cm) squares

(5) 1¾" × 3" (4.4 cm × 7.6 cm) rectangles

(21) 1¾" (4.4 cm) squares

For the house:

(2) 1¾" (4.4 cm) squares

From the red/cream bouquet print, cut:

For the stars:

(1) 3" (7.6 cm) square

(1) 2½" (6.4 cm) square

(10) 2" (5.1 cm) squares

(5) 1¾" × 3" (4.4 cm × 7.6 cm) rectangles

(21) 1¾" (4.4 cm) squares

For the house:

(1) 1¾" × 2½" (4.4 cm × 6.4 cm) rectangle

(1) 1⅛" × 1¼" (2.9 cm × 3.2 cm) rectangle

(1) 1" × 2½" (2.5 cm × 6.4 cm) strip

From the yellow flower print, cut:

For the stars:

(1) 3" (7.6 cm) square

(2) 2½"(6.4 cm) squares

(10) 2" (5.1 cm) squares

(6) 1¾" × 3" (4.4 cm × 7.6 cm) rectangles

(22) 1¾" (4.4 cm) squares

For the house:

(1) 1" × 1¼" (2.5 cm × 3.2 cm) rectangle

*From the red/brown stripe, fussy-cut the following, centered on the stripes:

(1) 1¾" × 4½" (4.4 cm × 11.4 cm) strip, on the lengthwise grain

(1) 1¾" × 2½" (4.4 cm × 6.4 cm) rectangle, on the crosswise grain

(1) 1¼" × 2½" (3.2 cm × 6.4 cm) strip, on the crosswise grain

(1) 1¼" × 1⅜" (3.2 cm × 3.5 cm) rectangle, on the crosswise grain

(1) 1⅛" × 1¼" (2.9 cm × 3.2 cm) rectangle, on the lengthwise grain

*From the tan/green prairie print, cut:

(2) 6⅛" × 15½" (15.6 cm × 39.4 cm) strips, on the crosswise grain

(2) 4¼"× 5⅜" (10.8 cm × 13.7 cm) rectangles, on the crosswise grain

(2) 1¾" (4.4 cm) squares

(1) 1" × 3½" (2.5 cm × 8.9 cm) strip, on the crosswise grain

(1) 1" × 2¼" (2.5 cm × 5.7 cm) strip, on the crosswise grain

From the gray floral, cut:

(1) 1¼" × 1⅞" (3.2 cm × 4.8 cm) rectangle

(1) 1" (2.5 cm) square

From the assorted pink, gold, green, blue, purple, and yellow florals and textures, cut:

(25) 3" (7.5 cm) squares

(24) 2½" (6.4 cm) squares

(194) 2" (5.1 cm) squares

(96) 1¾" × 3" (4.4 cm × 7.6 cm) rectangles

(432) 1¾" (4.4 cm) squares

From the tan solid, cut:

(2) 20½" × 55½" (52.1 cm × 141 cm) strips, on the lengthwise grain

(2) 15½" × 20½" (39.4 cm × 52.1 cm) rectangles

(84) 5½" (14 cm) squares

(112) 2" × 2½" (5.1 cm × 6.4 cm) rectangles

(112) 2" (5.1 cm) squares

(168) 1¾" × 3" (4.4 cm × 7.6 cm) rectangles

(336) 1¾" (4.4 cm) squares

(10) 2¼" (5.7 cm) × WOF strips for the binding

*See Using Directional Fabrics in Chapter 1.

PIECING THE HOUSE BLOCK
Finished size: 15" (38 cm) square

Note fabric orientation while piecing this block.

1. Referring to **FIGURE 1**, draw a diagonal line on the wrong side of (1) 1¾" (4.4 cm) red/beige vine print square and (1) 1¾" (4.4 cm) tan/green prairie print square. Set a square on one end of a 1¾" × 4½" (4.4 cm × 11.4 cm) striped strip as shown, right sides together and edges aligned. Stitch on the line. Repeat on the opposite end of the rectangle as shown. Trim excess fabric, then open and press to complete the roof unit.

2. Referring to **FIGURE 2**, position a 1¾" (4.4 cm) tan/green square as shown, then draw a diagonal line on the wrong side of the fabric. Set the square on a 1¾" (4.4 cm) red/beige vine print square, right sides together and edges aligned. Stitch on the line. Trim the excess fabric, then open and press to make the roof square.

3. Referring to **FIGURE 3**, join the 3½" (8.9 cm) tan/green prairie print strip, the 1" (2.5 cm) gray floral square, and the 2¼" (5.7 cm) tan/green prairie print strip to make the sky unit. Sew the pieced square to the roof unit to complete the roof strip. Sew the 1⅛" × 1¼" (2.9 cm × 3.2 cm) red/cream bouquet print rectangle to the top of the 1¼"× 1⅞" (3.2 cm × 4.8 cm) gray floral rectangle, then add the 1¾" × 2½" (4.4 cm × 6.4 cm) red/cream bouquet rectangle to the left and the 1" × 2½" (2.5 cm × 6.4 cm) red/cream strip to the right to make the front of the house. In a similar manner, sew the 1¼" × 1⅜" (3.2 cm × 3.5 cm) striped rectangle to the top of the 1" × 1¼" (2.5 cm × 3.2 cm) yellow flower print rectangle. Add the 1⅛" × 1¼" (2.9 cm × 3.2 cm) striped rectangle to the bottom to make the window unit. Sew the striped 1¼" × 2½" (3.2 cm × 6.4 cm) rectangle to the left and the striped 1¾" × 2½" (4.4 cm × 6.4 cm) rectangle to the right to complete the side of the house. Join the front and side of the house. Add the roof strip, then the sky unit.

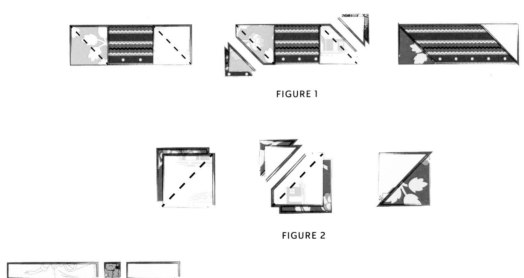

FIGURE 1

FIGURE 2

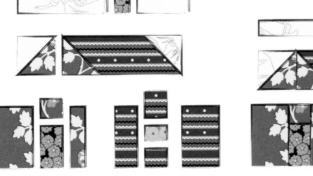
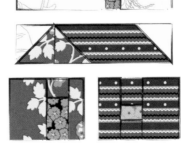

FIGURE 3

FIGURE 4

4. Referring to **FIGURE 4**, sew a 4¼"× 5⅜" (10.8 cm × 13.7 cm) tan/green prairie print rectangle to each side of the block center, then sew a 6⅛" × 15½" (15.6 cm × 39.4 cm) tan/green prairie print strip to the top and bottom to complete the house block.

MAKING THE SAWTOOTH STAR BLOCKS
Finished size: 5" (12.7 cm) square

5. Referring to **FIGURE 5**, draw a diagonal line on the wrong side of a 1¾" (4.4 cm) assorted square. Place the marked square on a tan 1¾" × 3" (4.4 cm × 7.6 cm) rectangle, right sides together and edges aligned. Stitch on the drawn line. Trim the excess fabric, then open and press. Repeat on the opposite end of the rectangle with another 1¾" (4.4 cm) assorted square to make 1 pieced rectangle. Make 168 pieced rectangles (set 56 aside for use in the Puzzle Star blocks).

6. Referring to **FIGURE 6**, sew 3 rows using (4) 1¾" (4.4 cm) tan squares, 4 pieced rectangles, and (1) 3" (7.6 cm) assorted square. Stitch the rows together to complete 1 Sawtooth Star block. Make 28.

Make 168

Pieced Rectangle

FIGURE 5

Make 28

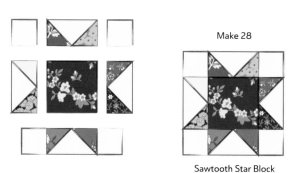

Sawtooth Star Block

FIGURE 6

MAKING THE TWIRLING STAR BLOCKS
Finished size: 5" (12.7 cm) square

7. Draw a diagonal line on the wrong side of a 2" (5.1 cm) assorted square. Referring to **FIGURE 7**, place the marked square on a 2" × 2½" (5.1 cm × 6.4 cm) tan rectangle, right sides together and edges aligned. Stitch on the drawn line. Trim the excess fabric, then

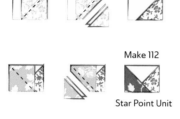

Make 112

Star Point Unit

FIGURE 7

open and press. Repeat on the opposite end of the rectangle with another 2" (5.1 cm) assorted square to make a star point unit. Make 112 star point units.

8. Referring to **FIGURE 8**, sew 3 rows using (4) 2" (5.1 cm) tan squares, 4 star point units, and (1) 2½" (6.4 cm) assorted square as shown. Stitch the rows together to complete a Twirling Star block. Make 28.

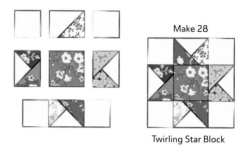

Make 28

Twirling Star Block

FIGURE 8

MAKING THE PUZZLE STAR BLOCKS
Finished size: 5" (12.7 cm) square

9. Referring to **FIGURE 9**, draw a diagonal line on the wrong side of a 1¾" (4.4 cm) tan square. Place the marked square on an 1¾" × 3" (4.5 cm × 7.6 cm) assorted rectangle, right sides together and edges aligned. Stitch on the drawn line. Trim the excess fabric, then open and press. Repeat on the opposite end of the rectangle with a 1¾" (4.4 cm) assorted square to make 1 side rectangle. Make 56. Reversing the orientation and placement of the assorted and tan squares, use the same technique to make 56 total reversed side rectangles (**FIGURE 10**).

10. Referring to **FIGURE 11**, sew 1 side rectangle and 1 reversed side rectangle together as shown to make a side unit. Make 2 and sew them together to make the middle row of the block. Use (4) 1¾" (4.4 cm) tan squares and 2 pieced rectangles (see step 5) to make the top and bottom rows, then sew the 3 rows together to complete 1 Puzzle Star block. Make 28.

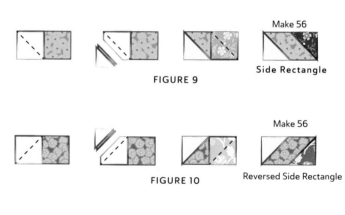

Make 56

Side Rectangle

FIGURE 9

Make 56

Reversed Side Rectangle

FIGURE 10

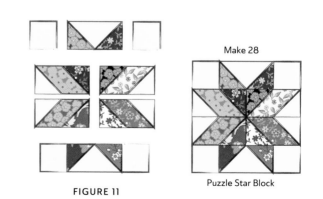

Make 28

FIGURE 11

Puzzle Star Block

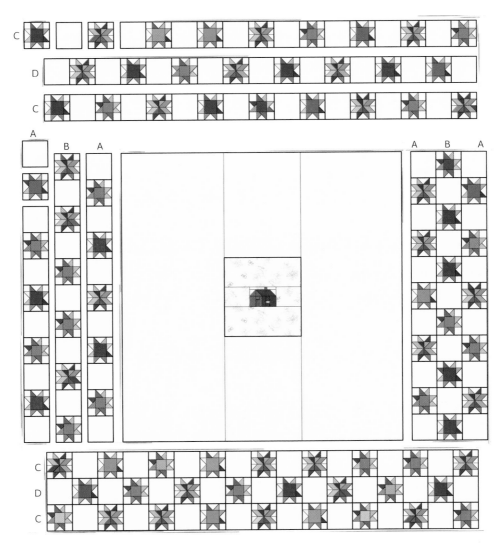

ASSEMBLY DIAGRAM

ASSEMBLING THE QUILT TOP
Refer to the **Assembly Diagram** throughout assembly.

11. Sew (1) 15½" × 20½" (39.4 × 52.1 cm) tan solid rectangle to the top, and the other to the bottom, of the house block. Stitch (1) 20½" × 55½" (52.1 × 141 cm) tan solid strip to each side of the house panel to complete the quilt top center.

12. Sew 4 vertical A Rows with (6) 5½" (14 cm) tan squares and 5 assorted star blocks each, alternating. Stitch 2 vertical B Rows with 6 assorted star blocks and (5) 5½" (14 cm) tan squares each, alternating. Sew together 2 A rows and 1 B row to make a side border strip. Make 2 side border strips and sew one to each side of the quilt center.

13. Sew 4 horizontal C Rows with 9 assorted star blocks and (8) 5½" (14 cm) tan squares each, alternating. Sew 2 D rows with (9) 5½" (14 cm) tan squares and 8 assorted blocks each, alternating. Stitch 2 C rows and 1 D row together to make a border strip. Make 2 border strips, and sew 1 to the top and 1 to the bottom of the quilt center to complete the quilt top.

FINISHING
14. Piece the quilt backing, being sure to make it at least 8" (20.3 cm) longer and wider than the quilt top. Layer the backing (wrong-side up), the batting, then the quilt top (right-side up) and baste them together.

15. Quilt as desired, then bind with the tan solid. The featured quilt has a star stitched in each tan square and a field of stars quilted in the area around the house.

MERRY TRAVELS

The Ingalls family did a lot of traveling. Sitting in the covered wagon or walking alongside the turning wheels, Laura journeyed from Wisconsin to Kansas and back again, before heading west to Minnesota. From Minnesota, the family traveled first to Iowa and then to South Dakota, where they settled happily. During these journeys, the wagon rolled across plains, over dirt roads, and through forests, steadily eating up the miles. And while hardships were inevitable in the *Little House* books, I imagine there was laughter and fun along the trail.

In this quilt, the larger block seems to be merrily rolling along, with happy feet and a good pace. You'll notice that these blocks travel in both directions, both to and from Kansas. I like this quilt best when it's laid horizontally across a bed. I can just see the wagon traveling back and forth across the plains.

MATERIALS

4 yards (3.7 m) tan/multicolor mini-dot for the Footed Wheel blocks and setting triangles

5/8 yard (0.6 m) each red bouquet print, brown bouquet print, brown/tan vine print, and red/tan vine print for the blocks

7/8 yard (0.8 m) cream wheat print for the Pinwheel blocks

3½ yards (3.2 m) brown/gold/red wallpaper stripe for the sashing strips, border, and binding*

7 yards (6.4 m) backing fabric

92" × 102" (233.7 cm × 259.1 cm) batting

* **Note:** The wallpaper stripe yardage is based on a fabric that allows 8 lengthwise strips (4⅛" [10.5 cm] wide and centered on a stripe) to be cut from 1 width of fabric. If your chosen fabric allows for fewer strips to be cut from 1 width of fabric, you'll need to purchase more.

Finished size: 83¼" × 92⅝" (211.4 cm × 235.3 cm)
Pieced by Laura Stone Roberts
Quilted by Donna Smith

CUTTING INSTRUCTIONS

For best use of fabric, cut strips and patches in the order listed.

From the tan/multicolor mini-dot, cut:
(6) 18¼" (46.4 cm) squares; cut twice diagonally to make 24 quarter-square triangles
(6) 9⅜" (23.8 cm) squares; cut diagonally to make 12 half-square triangles
(60) 3⅞" (9.7 cm) squares
(60) 3½" × 6½" (8.9 cm x 16.5 cm) rectangles

From the red bouquet print, cut:
(8) 7¼" (18.4 cm) squares
(18) 3⅜" (8.6 cm) squares

From the brown bouquet print, cut:
(7) 7¼" (18.5) squares
(18) 3⅜"(8.6 cm) squares

From the brown/tan vine print, cut:
(32) 3½" (8.9 cm) squares
(16) 3⅜" (8.6 cm) squares

From the red/tan vine print, cut:
(28) 3½" (8.9 cm) squares
(16) 3⅜" (8.6 cm) squares

From the cream wheat print, cut:
(68) 3⅜" (8.6 cm) squares

From the brown/gold/red wallpaper stripe, cut:
(6) 4⅛" × 90" (10.5 cm × 228.6 cm) strips, on the lengthwise grain, centered on a floral stripe
(2) 4⅛" × 86" (10.5 cm × 218.4 cm) strips, on the lengthwise grain, centered on a floral stripe
(10) 2¼" (5.7 cm) × WOF (width-of-fabric) strips for the binding

From the backing fabric, cut:
(2) 40" × 92" (101.5 cm × 233.7 cm) strips
(2) 21" × 47" (53.3 cm × 119.4 cm) strips, on the lengthwise grain

PIECING THE FOOTED WHEEL BLOCKS
Finished block size: 12" (30.5 cm) square

Note the fabric orientation while piecing this block.

1. Draw a diagonal line on the wrong side of each 3⅞" (9.7 cm) tan/multicolor mini-dot square. Referring to **FIGURE 1**, place 2 marked squares on opposite corners of a 7¼" (18.4 cm) red bouquet print square, right sides together and edges aligned. (The drawn lines will connect to make a center line, and the squares will overlap where they meet in the middle.) Sew a ¼" (6 mm) seam on each side of the marked lines, then cut apart on the lines. Open and press the small triangles. Place a marked mini-dot square on the red bouquet corner of each unit, aligning as shown, with right sides together and edges aligned. Sew a ¼" (6 mm) seam allowance on each side of the marked lines and cut apart. Open and press the small triangles to complete 4 red/tan mini-dot Flying Geese units. Make 32. In the same manner, use the remaining 3⅞" (9.7 cm) mini-dot squares and the 7¼" (18.4 cm) brown bouquet print squares to make 28 brown/mini-dot Flying Geese units.

2. Referring to **FIGURE 2**, draw a diagonal line on the wrong side of each brown/tan vine print and each 3½" (8.9 cm) red/tan vine print square. Place a marked brown square on a 3½" × 6½" (8.9 cm × 16.5 cm) mini-dot rectangle, right sides together and edges

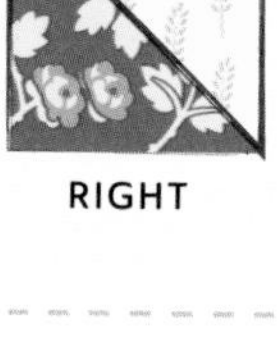

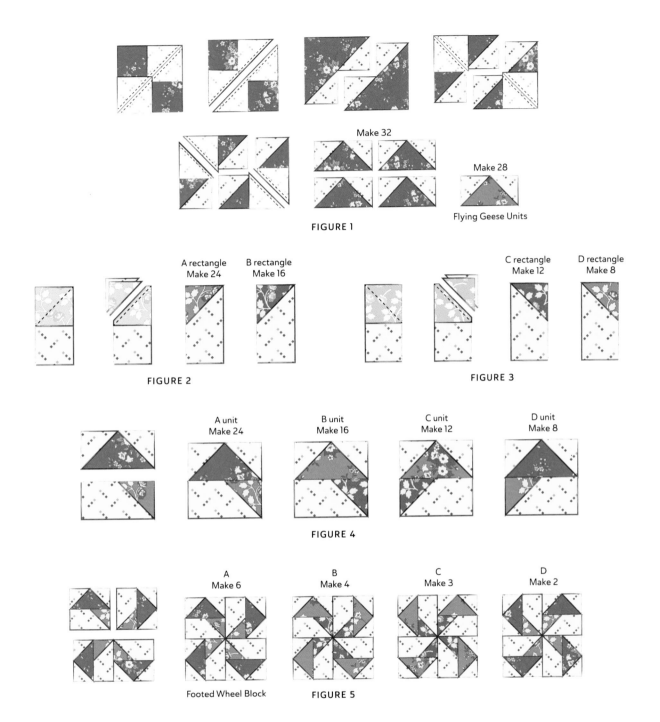

Make 32

Make 28

Flying Geese Units

FIGURE 1

A rectangle
Make 24

B rectangle
Make 16

C rectangle
Make 12

D rectangle
Make 8

FIGURE 2

FIGURE 3

A unit
Make 24

B unit
Make 16

C unit
Make 12

D unit
Make 8

FIGURE 4

A
Make 6

B
Make 4

C
Make 3

D
Make 2

Footed Wheel Block

FIGURE 5

aligned. Stitch on the drawn line, then trim the excess fabric. Press the triangle open to make 1 brown/tan mini-dot pieced A rectangle. Make 24. In the same manner, make 16 red/tan mini-dot pieced B rectangles. Orienting the marked squares as shown in **FIGURE 3**, make 12 red/tan mini-dot pieced C rectangles and 8 brown/tan mini-dot D rectangles.

3. Referring to **FIGURE 4**, sew together 1 red/tan mini-dot Flying Goose unit and 1 pieced A rectangle to make an A unit. Make 24. Stitch the remaining Flying Geese units and pieced rectangles together to make the B, C, and D units in the quantities shown.

4. Sew together 4 A units to make 1 Footed Wheel block A (**FIGURE 5**). Make 6. In the same manner, make the B, C, and D Footed Wheel blocks in the quantities shown.

PIECING THE PINWHEEL BLOCKS
Finished size: 5" (12.7 cm)

5. Draw a diagonal line on the wrong side of each 3⅜" (8.6 cm) cream print square. Referring to **FIGURE 6**, place a marked square on a 3⅜" (8.6 cm) red bouquet print square, right sides together and edges aligned. Sew a ¼" (6 mm) seam on each side of the marked line, then cut apart on the line. Open and press to make 2 pieced squares E. Make 36. In the same manner, make pieced squares F, G, and H in the fabric combinations and quantities shown.

6. Referring to **FIGURE 7**, sew 4 matching pieced squares together as shown to make a Pinwheel block. Make Pinwheel blocks E–H in the quantities shown.

ASSEMBLING THE QUILT TOP
Refer to the **Assembly Diagram** throughout assembly.

7. To make the first Footed Wheel blocks row, sew together 3 Footed Wheel blocks A, 2 Footed Wheel blocks B, and (8) 18¼" (46.4 cm) mini-dot quarter-square setting triangles, alternating the blocks as shown. Sew (4) 9⅜" (23.8 cm) mini-dot half-square triangles to the ends. Repeat to make the third Footed Wheel blocks row.

8. To make the middle Footed Wheel blocks row, sew together 3 Footed Wheel blocks C, 2 Footed Wheel blocks D, and (8) 18¼" (46.4 cm) mini-dot quarter-square triangles, alternating the blocks as shown. Sew (4) 9⅜" (23.8 cm) mini-dot half-square triangles to the ends.

9. To make the first Pinwheel blocks row, sew together 5 E blocks, 4 F blocks, 4 G blocks, and 4 H blocks in the order shown. To make the second Pinwheel blocks row, sew together 5 F blocks, 4 G blocks, 4 H blocks, and 4 E blocks in the order shown.

10. Measure the lengths of the 5 block rows, from raw edge to raw edge. Add the 5 measurements together, then divide by 5 to get the average row length. Trim the (6) 4⅛" × 90" (10.5 cm x 228.6 cm) wallpaper stripe strips to this length. Sew the strips and the rows together in the order shown, aligning the top and bottom edges.

E
Make 36

F
Make 36

G
Make 32

H
Make 32

FIGURE 6

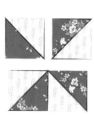
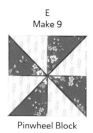

E
Make 9

Pinwheel Block

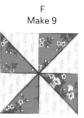

F
Make 9

G
Make 8

H
Make 9

FIGURE 7

ASSEMBLY DIAGRAM

11. Measure the quilt width through the middle from edge to edge. Trim the 4⅛" × 86" (10.5 cm × 218.4 cm) wallpaper stripe strips to this length and sew to the top and bottom of the quilt.

FINISHING
12. Sew the 21" (53.3 cm) backing strips together end-to-end to make the center strip of the backing. Sew a 92" (233.7 cm) backing strip to either side of the pieced strip. Trim the edges even to complete the backing. Layer the backing (wrong-side up), the batting, and quilt top (right-side up), and baste them together.

13. Quilt as desired, then bind.

BRAIDS, BONNETS, AND BOWS

In the latter half of the century, American pioneer girls and their mothers wore a hat or bonnet whenever they stepped outside. Under their bonnets, girls wore their hair in long braids tied with ribbons, while their mothers had braids of their own, worn in a plain bun or a fancier updo.

I'm sure that I could look at an array of bonnets from Walnut Grove and know which one was Laura's and which was Mrs. Oleson's. I can picture Ma's sweet ladylike bonnet and Nellie's slightly gauche one. But now it's your turn to imagine what the ladies and girls of the *Little House* books would be wearing. In making this quilt, you get to design the bonnets by choosing which two fabrics go into each one and what color braid belongs around each bonnet block. Maybe Mary's bonnet would be a soft brown with gold ties to show off her blonde braids. Perhaps a green bonnet with a long yellow ribbon would go home with Miss Beadle. It's up to you!

MATERIALS

2¾ yards (2.5 m) tan girl print for Bow block backgrounds

1⅞ yards (1.7 m) tan solid for Bonnet block backgrounds

⅝ yard (0.6 m) each of 3 assorted brown florals/textures, 3 assorted yellow/gold florals/textures, and 3 assorted black/gray florals/textures for the braided block frames

⅜ yard (0.3 m) each of a medium pink floral and a light blue texture for the pieced bows

¼ yard (0.2 m) each of medium purple, pale yellow, and medium green florals for the pieced bows

Fat eighth (9" × 21" [22.9 cm × 53.3 cm]) each pale pink and small navy-and-yellow florals for the pieced bows

9" × 10" (22.9 cm × 25.4 cm) rectangle each of dark purple texture, medium yellow floral, and light green floral for the pieced bows

10" (25.4 cm) square each of 13 assorted florals and textures for the bonnets and their ribbons

3 yards (2.7 m) paper-backed fusible web (at least 17" [43.2 cm] wide) for the appliqué

4¾ yards (4.3 m) backing fabric

⅝ yard (0.6 m) lavender floral for the binding

79" (200.7 cm) square batting

Bow and bonnet templates (see Chapter 3)

Finished size: 70½" (179.1 cm) square
Pieced and appliquéd by Kathryn Patterson
Quilted by Donna Smith

CUTTING INSTRUCTIONS

Cut the pieces below in the order listed. Cutting instructions for the bonnets and ribbons are with the templates in the back of the book. Templates are printed reversed and without turn-under allowances to use with paper-backed fusible web. Each bonnet uses two fabrics: one for the hat, the other for the accompanying ribbon. For example, when cutting out the templates for a Ruffle Bonnet, cut the K template from one fabric and the L, M, N, O, and P templates from a second fabric. You can cut one bonnet and one ribbon from each 10" (25.4 cm) square.

From the tan girl print, cut:
(12) 3" × 14½" (7.6 × 36.8 cm) strips
(12) 2" × 14½" (5.1 cm × 36.8 cm) strips
(12) 4½" × 5½" (11.4 cm × 14 cm) rectangles
(24) 4" × 4½" (10.2 cm × 11.4 cm) rectangles
(12) 2½" × 4" (6.4 cm × 10.2 cm) rectangles
(24) 2" × 4½" (5.1 cm × 11.4 cm) strips
(12) 2½" × 3½" (6.4 cm × 8.9 cm) rectangles
(24) 2½" (6.4 cm) squares
(12) 2" × 2½" (5.1 cm × 6.4 cm) rectangles
(84) 1½" × 2½" (3.8 cm × 6.4 cm) rectangles
(240) 1½" (3.8 cm) squares

From the tan solid, cut:
(13) 12" (30.5 cm) squares

From the 3 assorted brown florals/textures, cut:
A total of: (5) 4" (10.2 cm) squares; cut twice diagonally to make 20 quarter-square triangles
From each fabric: (256) 1" × 2½" (1.3 cm × 6.4 cm) strips

From the 3 assorted yellow/gold florals/textures, cut:
A total of: (4) 4" (10.2 cm) squares; cut each in half twice diagonally to make 16 quarter-square triangles
From each fabric: (205) 1" × 2½" (2.5 cm × 6.4 cm) strips

From the 3 assorted black/gray florals/textures, cut:
A total of: (4) 4" (10.2 cm) squares; cut each in half twice diagonally to make 16 quarter-square triangles
From each fabric, cut: (205) 1" × 2½" (2.5 cm × 6.4 cm) strips

From both the medium pink floral and light blue texture, cut:
(3) 1½" × 5½" (3.8 cm × 14 cm) strips
(9) 1½" × 4½" (3.8 cm × 11.4 cm) strips
(18) 1½" × 2½" (3.8 cm × 6.4 cm) strips
(33) 1½" (3.8 cm) squares

From each of the medium purple, pale yellow, and medium green florals, cut:
(2) 1½" × 5½" (3.8 cm × 14 cm) strips
(6) 1½" × 4½" (3.8 cm × 11.4 cm) strips
(12) 1½" × 2½" (3.8 cm × 6.4 cm) strips
(22) 1½" (3.8 cm) squares

From both the pale pink and small navy/yellow florals, cut:
(15) 1½" × 2½" (3.8 cm × 6.4 cm) strips
(12) 1½" (3.8 cm) squares

From each of the dark purple texture, medium yellow floral, and light green floral fabrics, cut:
(10) 1½" × 2½" (3.8 cm × 6.4 cm) strips
(8) 1½" (3.8 cm) squares

From the lavender floral, cut:
(8) 2¼" (5.7 cm) × WOF (width-of-fabric) strips for the binding

From the backing fabric, cut:
(2) 80" (203.2 cm) × WOF strips

HALF-PINT TIP
Appliqué Without Stiffness

To make large appliqué shapes less stiff, cut out the center of the fusible web shape before ironing it onto the fabric. Trace the template onto the paper side of the fusible web and cut it out, leaving a small margin outside the traced line. Next, cut an opening ½" (1.3 cm) inside the traced line. Fuse this narrow shape to the wrong side of the fabric as shown, then cut out the fabric shape as usual.

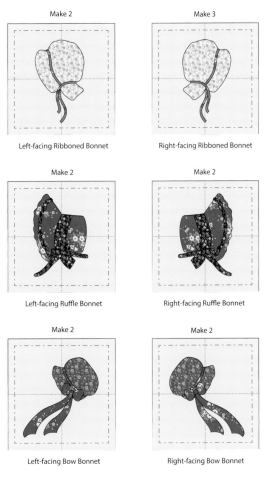

Make 2   Make 3

Left-facing Ribboned Bonnet   Right-facing Ribboned Bonnet

Make 2   Make 2

Left-facing Ruffle Bonnet   Right-facing Ruffle Bonnet

Make 2   Make 2

Left-facing Bow Bonnet   Right-facing Bow Bonnet

FIGURE 1

APPLIQUÉING THE BONNET BLOCKS
Finished block size: 14" (35.5 cm) square

Follow the manufacturer's instructions for using the fusible web. Read the Half-Pint Tip, Appliqué without Stiffness, before appliquéing the bonnets. **Note**: The 12" (30.5 cm) tan background squares are cut oversized to allow for shrinkage during appliqué.

1. Trace all Templates A/Ar–D/Dr on the paper side of the fusible web. Cut the templates apart, leaving a small margin beyond the drawn lines. Fuse the templates to the wrong side of the appropriate 10" (25.4 cm) squares of fabric and cut them out on the drawn lines. Each bonnet uses 1 fabric for the bonnet itself and 1 contrasting fabric for the ribbons. Mix and match as desired, but make a plan before cutting. Finger press 1 of the 12" (30.5 cm) tan solid squares in half on both the length and the width, as well as on both diagonals to find the center point. Referring to **FIGURE 1** and using the fold lines as a guide, position an A template, plus matching B, C, and D templates in alphabetical order on the tan square as shown in the Ribboned Bonnet template **Assembly Diagram** in Chapter 3. Keep in mind that the square will be trimmed to 10½" (26.4 cm) square. Fuse the templates in place. Edgestitch the appliqué using a machine straight or decorative stitch of your choice. Centering the appliqué, trim the block to 10½" (26.4 cm) square to complete 1 left-facing Ribboned Bonnet square. In the same manner, make a total of 2 left-facing Ribboned Bonnet squares and 3 right-facing Ribboned Bonnet squares.

2. In the same manner, use the E/Er–P/Pr templates to make 2 right-facing and 2 left-facing Bow Bonnet blocks as well as 2 right-facing and 2 left-facing Ruffle Bonnet blocks as shown on the template pages.

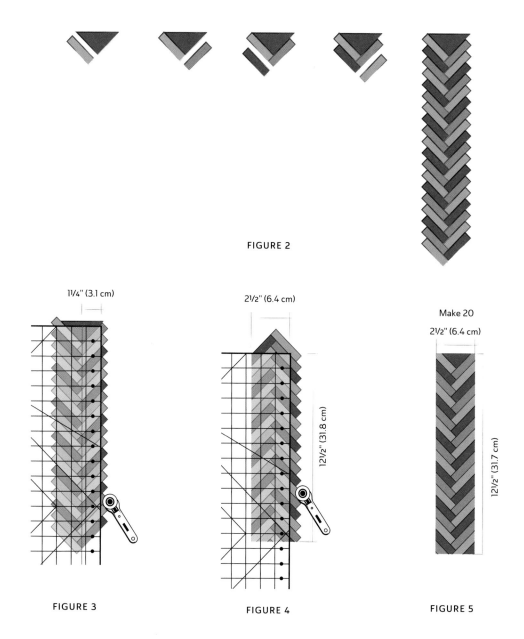

FIGURE 2

1¼" (3.1 cm)

FIGURE 3

2½" (6.4 cm)

12½" (31.8 cm)

FIGURE 4

Make 20

2½" (6.4 cm)

12½" (31.7 cm)

FIGURE 5

MAKING AND ADDING THE BRAIDED BLOCK FRAMES

3. Referring to **FIGURE 2** and aligning strips as shown, sew (1) 1" × 2½" (2.5 cm × 6.4 cm) assorted brown strip to the side of a 4" (10.2 cm) quarter-square triangle of a different assorted brown; press open. Sew (1) 1" × 2½" (2.5 cm × 6.4 cm) strip of the third brown fabric to the opposite side of the triangle; press open. Continue adding strips in the same manner, keeping the 3 fabrics in sequence, until 37 strips have been used.

4. To trim the pieced strip (**FIGURE 3**), align the 1¼" (3.1 cm) ruler line with the center of the pieced strip, between the strip seam intersections, and the top edge of the ruler approximately ½" (1.3 cm) below the edge of the triangle. Trim the right *and* top edges of the pieced strip.

5. Referring to **FIGURE 4**, rotate the strip and align the 2½" (6.4 cm) ruler line with the freshly trimmed side edge and the 12½" (31.7 cm) ruler line with the freshly trimmed end of the strip. Trim the remaining edges to complete 1 brown braided strip (**FIGURE 5**). Make 20. (You will have a few fabric strips left over.)

Make 16   Make 16

FIGURE 6

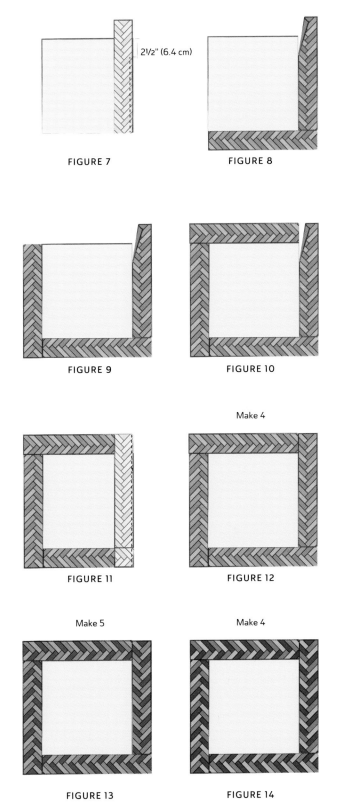

2½" (6.4 cm)

FIGURE 7

FIGURE 8

FIGURE 9

FIGURE 10

FIGURE 11

Make 4

FIGURE 12

Make 5

FIGURE 13

Make 4

FIGURE 14

6. Referring to **FIGURE 6**, and in the same manner, use the assorted yellow/gold and the assorted black/gray triangles and strips to make 16 braided strips of each color group. You will have a few fabric strips left over.

7. Note the orientation of the braided strips throughout. Beginning 2" (5.1 cm) below the upper right corner of any appliquéd square, stitch the first seam as shown (**FIGURE 7**). Open and press the partial seam, creating an edge at the bottom that is the same length as a braided strip. Working counterclockwise, sew the bottom, left, and top braided strips to the appliquéd square, pressing open after each addition (**FIGURES 8-10**).

8. Referring to **FIGURE 11**, fold the first strip back over the block and lower the needle at the end of the partial seam. Backstitch 1 or 2 stitches, then sew from this point to the top edge of the block. Make 4 blocks with yellow/gold braided frames (**FIGURE 12**). In the same manner, make 5 blocks with brown braided frames and 4 blocks with black/gray braided frames (**FIGURES 13-14**).

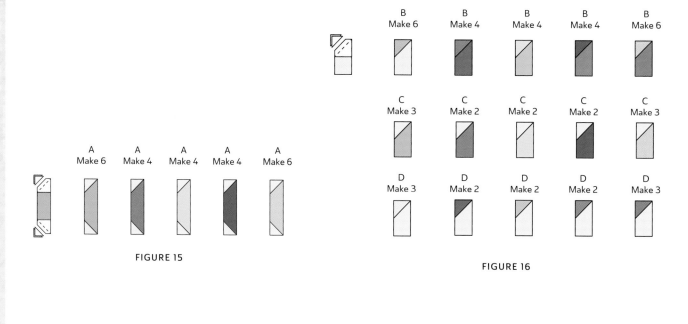

B
Make 6   Make 4   Make 4   Make 4   Make 6

C
Make 3   Make 2   Make 2   Make 2   Make 3

D
Make 3   Make 2   Make 2   Make 2   Make 3

FIGURE 16

A
Make 6   Make 4   Make 4   Make 4   Make 6

FIGURE 15

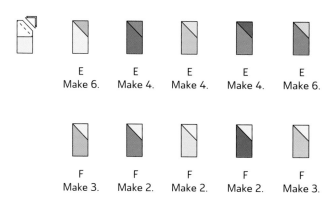

E
Make 6.   Make 4.   Make 4.   Make 4.   Make 6.

F
Make 3.   Make 2.   Make 2.   Make 2.   Make 3.

FIGURE 17

MAKING THE BOW BLOCKS
Finished block size: 14" (35.6 cm) square

9. Draw a diagonal line on the wrong side of a 1½" (3.8 cm) tan girl print square. Place the marked square on a 1½" × 4½" (3.8 cm × 11.4 cm) medium pink strip, right sides together and aligning the edges (**FIGURE 15**). Sew on the marked line. Trim the excess fabric, then open and press. Repeat on the opposite end of the strip to make 1 pieced strip A. Make the remaining A strips in the fabrics and quantities shown.

10. Referring to **FIGURES 16** and **17**, use 1½" (3.8 cm) squares, 1½" × 2½" (3.8 cm × 6.4 cm) rectangles,

and the same stitch-and-flip technique to make the B, C, D, E, and F pieced rectangles in the fabric arrangements and quantities shown.

11. In the same manner, and noting the orientation of the squares, use 1½" (3.8 cm) squares, 1½" × 2½" (6.4 cm × 6.4 cm) rectangles, and 2½" × 3½" (6.4 cm × 8.9 cm) rectangles to make the G, H, I, J, K and L pieced rectangles in the fabric arrangements and quantities shown (**FIGURES 18-20**).

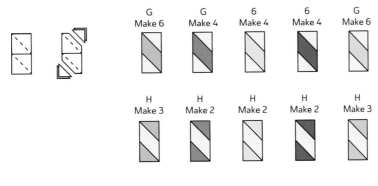

G
Make 6

G
Make 4

6
Make 4

6
Make 4

G
Make 6

H
Make 3

H
Make 2

H
Make 2

H
Make 2

H
Make 3

FIGURE 18

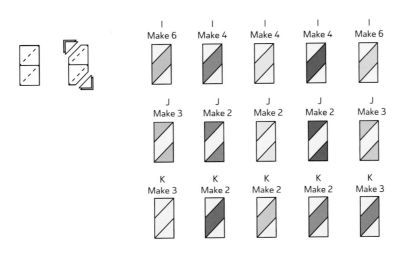

I
Make 6

I
Make 4

I
Make 4

I
Make 4

I
Make 6

J
Make 3

J
Make 2

J
Make 2

J
Make 2

J
Make 3

K
Make 3

K
Make 2

K
Make 2

K
Make 2

K
Make 3

FIGURE 19

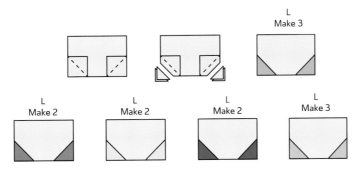

L
Make 3

L
Make 2

L
Make 2

L
Make 2

L
Make 3

FIGURE 20

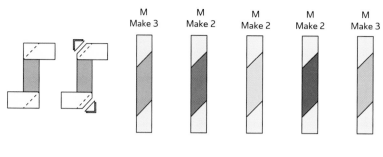

FIGURE 21

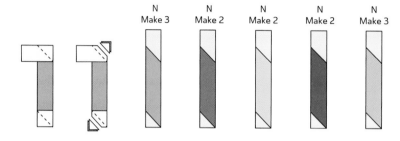

FIGURE 22

12. Referring to **FIGURES 21** and **22**, in the same manner and noting the orientation of the tan patches, use 1½" × 2½" (3.8 cm × 6.4 cm) rectangles, 1½" × 4½" (3.8 cm × 11.4 cm) strips, 1½" × 5½" (3.8 cm × 14 cm) strips, and 1½" (3.8 cm) squares to make pieced strips M and N in the fabrics and quantities shown.

13. Use the stitch-and-flip technique (see the Half-Pint Tip in the Big Sky quilt directions) to add 1½" (3.8 cm) squares (in the fabrics shown) to 2½" × 4" (6.4 cm × 10.2 cm) tan rectangles to make pieced O rectangles in the fabrics and quantities shown (**FIGURE 23**).

14. Referring to **FIGURE 24** and following the seaming order shown, sew together tan rectangles and squares, medium and pale pink squares, and pink/tan pieced strips and rectangles to make 6 bow sections. Referring to **FIGURE 25**, sew the 6 sections together to make the bow, then add a 3" × 14½" (7.5 × 36.8 cm) tan strip to the top and a 2" × 14½" (5.1 cm × 36.8 cm) tan strip to the bottom to complete 1 pink Bow block (**FIGURE 26**). Make 3 pink Bow blocks. In the same manner, make 2 purple, 2 yellow, 2 green, and 3 blue Bow blocks.

15. In the same manner and referring to **FIGURES 24-26**, make the purple, yellow, green, and blue Bow blocks.

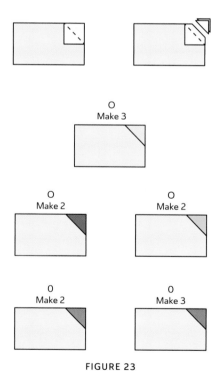

FIGURE 23

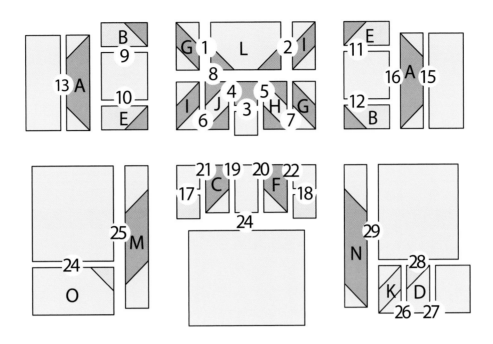

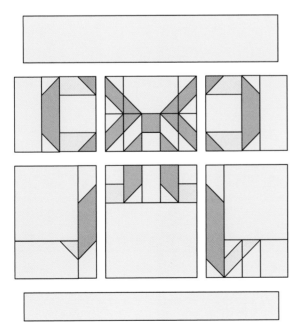

FIGURE 24

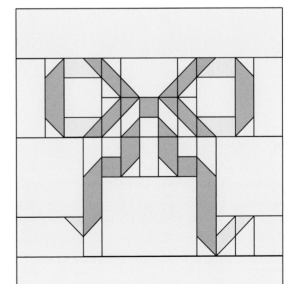

FIGURE 25

Make 3 pink, 2 purple, 2 yellow, 2 green, and 3 blue Bow blocks

FIGURE 26

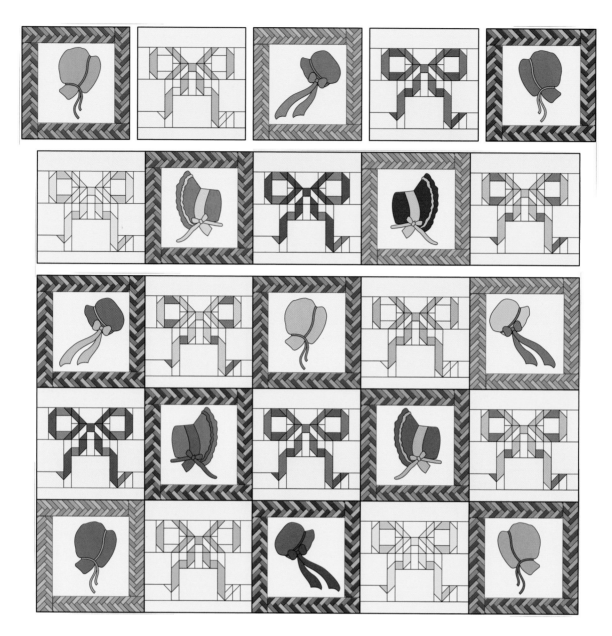

ASSEMBLY DIAGRAM

ASSEMBLING THE QUILT TOP

Refer to the **Assembly Diagram** throughout assembly.

15. Lay out all the blocks on a design wall or another large flat surface, arranging them as you wish. Sew 3 rows with 3 Bonnet blocks and 2 Bow blocks each. Sew 2 rows with 3 Bow blocks and 2 Bonnet blocks each. Stitch the rows together, alternating, to complete the quilt top.

FINISHING

16. Piece the quilt backing, making sure it is at least 8" (20.3 cm) longer and wider than the quilt top. Layer the backing (wrong-side up), the batting, and the quilt top (right-side up), and baste them together.

17. Quilt as desired, then bind the quilt with the lavender floral strips.

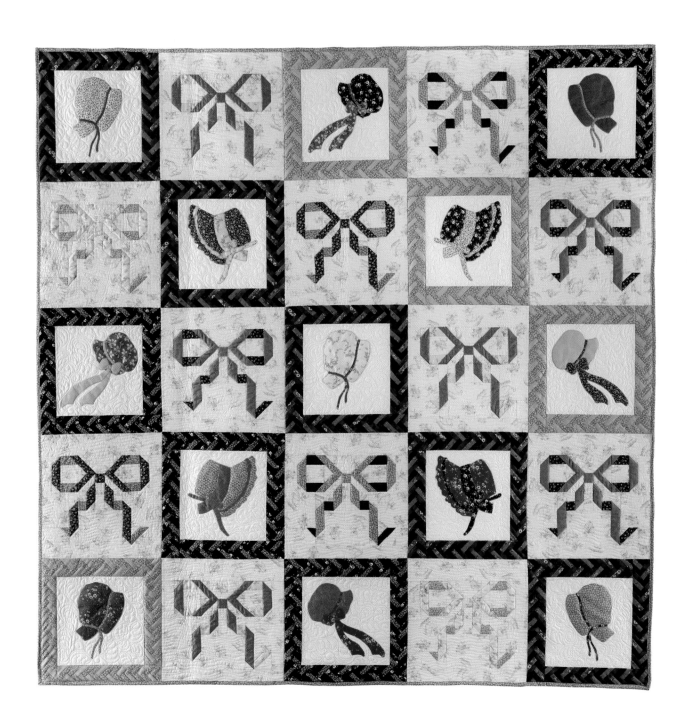

SCHOOLHOUSES AND SUNFLOWERS

This quilt celebrates two of the most important things in the life of the Ingalls family: the seasons and school.

For a pioneer family like Laura's, seasonal events formed the rhythm of life. Early spring meant maple syrup in *Little House in the Big Woods*, while early summer meant roses in *Little Town on the Prairie*. In *These Happy Golden Years*, winter brought sleigh rides. In *Farmer Boy*, autumn harvesting filled the home from cellar to attic with pumpkins and apples, peppers and beans, beechnuts and corn. Activities were also regulated by the seasons. If you're working all day to preserve produce, there's no time to quilt. But if snow keeps you indoors, then quilting is just the way to pass the day…unless it's time for school.

Few things signified civilization on the prairie like a schoolhouse. If a town was big enough for a schoolhouse, that meant there were enough children nearby to fill a schoolroom. For women like Ma, that meant friends, church services, and town gatherings. And, with two teachers in the family, it's no wonder that Laura Ingalls Wilder wrote so many stories centered around school.

One of the things I love about this quilt is that I can rotate it on my bed as the seasons change. Rather than list specific fabrics, I've mostly described the fabrics in this quilt by season. It's up to you to decide which colors to use. I suggest organizing your fabrics by season when cutting patches. You may wish to buy a fat quarter for each of your book border fabrics, then use the same fabrics in the Schoolhouse blocks. Please read through the entire materials list before purchasing fabric.

This quilt may look daunting, but none of the sewing is hard. Just go one step at a time, and you'll soon have a one-of-a-kind quilt. Be sure to check your ¼" (6mm) seam allowance for accuracy so all parts fit together well.

Finished size: 81½" (207 cm) square
Pieced by Laura Stone Roberts
Quilted by Donna Smith

MATERIALS

Read the introduction before buying fabric. When an entry calls for 4 assorted fabrics, choose 1 fabric for each season.

4 fat eighths (9" × 21" [22.9 cm × 53.3 cm]) assorted sky fabrics

(4) 6" × 7" (15.2 cm × 17.8 cm) rectangles assorted roof peak fabrics

4 fat eighths (9" × 21" [22.9 cm × 53.4 cm]) assorted wall fabrics

4" (10.2 cm) square gray texture fabric for bells

4 fat eighths (9" × 21" [22.9 cm × 53.3 cm]) assorted roof fabrics

(4) 5" × 7" (12.7 cm × 17.8 cm) rectangles assorted door fabrics

(4) 6" × 7" (15.2 cm × 17.8 cm) rectangles assorted window fabrics

4 fat eighths (9" × 21" [22.9 cm × 53.3 cm]) assorted ground fabrics

2⅜ yards (2.2 m) total assorted yellow, gold, and tan florals, prints, and textures for sunflowers

¾ yard (0.7 m) dark brown texture for sunflower centers

2 yards (1.8 m) tan/green prairie print for sunflower backgrounds

4 fat eighths (9" × 21" [22.9 cm × 53.3 cm]) each of spring, summer, autumn, and winter prints, florals, or textures for books

1 yard (0.9 m) light tan print for book backgrounds

1¾ yards (1.6 m) tan house print for inner and outer borders

6½ yards (6 m) backing fabric

¾ yard (0.7 m) fabric for binding

90" (231 cm) square batting

3" (7.6 cm) square paper-backed fusible web for the bells

Awl or large needle

Add-A-Quarter ruler

See-through template plastic

Templates A, B, Br (B reversed) and C (see Chapter 3)

Foundation Masters D-G (see Chapter 3)

CUTTING INSTRUCTIONS

For best use of fabric, cut the strips and patches in the order listed.

From each of the 4 assorted sky fabrics, cut:
(2) 4½" × 7½" (11.4 cm × 19.1 cm) rectangles
(2) 2½" × 6½" (6.4 cm × 16.5 cm) strips
(1) 1¾" (4.4 cm) square
(1) 1½" × 2½" (3.8 cm × 6.4 cm) rectangle
(2) 1½" (3.8 cm) squares

From each of the 4 roof peak fabrics, cut:
1 Template C*
(1) 1½" × 2½" (3.8 cm × 6.4 cm) rectangle

From each of the 4 wall fabrics, cut:
(2) 1¼" × 5¾" (3.2 cm × 14.6 cm) strips
(4) 1⅝" × 5¼" (4.1 cm × 13.3 cm) strips
(1) 1¼" × 5" (3.2 cm × 12.7 cm) strip
(2) 1¾" × 4¼"(4.4 cm × 10.8 cm) strips
(2) ⅞" × 2½" (2.2 cm × 6.4 cm) strips
(2) ⅞" × 1¾" (2.2 cm × 4.4 cm) strips

From the gray texture, cut:
4 Template A**

From each of the 4 roof fabrics, cut:
1 Template B*
1 Template Br*
(2) 4½" × 5" (11.4 cm × 12.7 cm) rectangles
(1) 1½" × 3½" (3.8 cm × 8.9 cm) strip

From each of the 4 door fabrics, cut:
(1) 3½" × 5¾" (8.9 cm × 14.6 cm) rectangle

From each of the 4 window fabrics, cut:
(2) 2" × 5¼" (5.1 cm × 13.3 cm) strips

From each of the 4 ground fabrics, cut:
(1) 2½" × 16½" (6.4 cm × 42 cm) strip
(2) 2½" × 4½" (6.4 cm × 11.4 cm) rectangles

From the assorted yellow, gold, and tan fabrics for sunflowers, cut a total of:
(40) 7¼" (18.4 cm) squares for FMs (Foundation Masters) D and E, area 1
(32) squares 3⅜" (8.6 cm) squares for FMs F and G, area 1

From the dark brown texture, cut
(40) 3½" × 4" (8.9 cm × 10.2 cm) rectangles, for FMs D and E, area 2
(32) 2½" × 3" (6.4 cm × 7.5 cm) rectangles for FMs F and G, area 2

From the tan/green prairie print, cut:
(40) 5" × 6" (12.7 cm × 15.2 cm) rectangles for FMs D and E, area 4
(32) 3¾" × 4¼" (9.5 cm × 10.8 cm) rectangles for FMs F and G, area 4
(40) 2¾" × 5" (7 cm × 12.7 cm) rectangles for FMs D and E, area 3
(32) 2" × 3½" (5.1 cm × 8.9 cm) rectangles for FMs F and G, area 3

From each of the 4 spring, 4 summer, 4 autumn, and 4 winter fabrics for books, cut:
(1) 8" × 20" (20.3 cm × 50.8 cm) strip

From the light tan print, cut:
(16) 2" × 20" (5.1 cm × 50.8 cm) strips
(16) 1½" × 20" (3.8 cm × 50.8 cm) strips

From the tan house print, cut:
(2) 4½" × 56½" (11.4 cm × 143.5 cm) strips, pieced from 3 WOF (width-of-fabric) strips***
(2) 4½" × 48½" (11.4 cm × 123.2 cm) strips, pieced from 3 WOF strips***
(2) 3" × 86" (7.6 cm × 218.4 cm) strips, pieced from 5 WOF strips****
(2) 3" × 80" (7.6 cm × 203.2 cm) strips, pieced from 4 WOF strips****

From the binding fabric, cut:
(9) 2¼" (5.7 cm) × WOF strips

From the backing fabric, cut:
(2) 40" × 90½" (101.5 cm × 229.9 cm) strips
(3) 11" × 30½" (27.9 cm × 77.5 cm) strips

*These template shapes are cut in step 3.
**Bell shapes are cut in step 2.
***These border strips are cut to the exact length to fit the subsequent pieced border.
****Strips include extra length for trimming.

HALF-PINT TIP
Measure as You Go

When you're just learning to quilt, measure each block and unit as you finish it to make sure it's the right size. If it's not, check to make sure you're using an accurate ¼" (6 mm) seam allowance and have pressed the seams completely open.

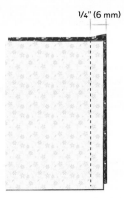

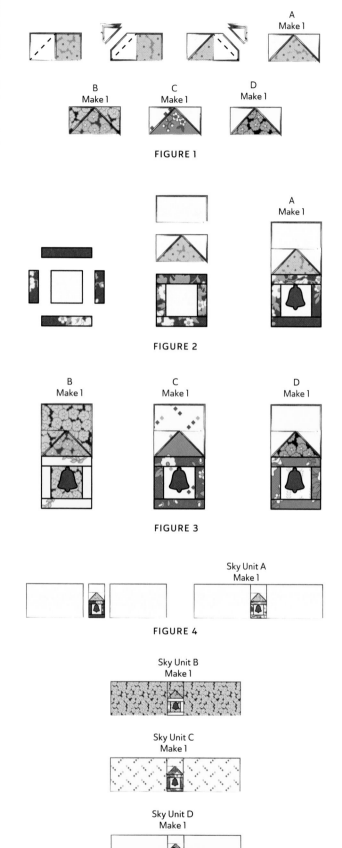

FIGURE 1

FIGURE 2

FIGURE 3

Sky Unit A
Make 1

FIGURE 4

Sky Unit B
Make 1

Sky Unit C
Make 1

Sky Unit D
Make 1

FIGURE 5

PIECING THE SCHOOLHOUSE BLOCKS
Finished block size: 16" (40.6 cm) square

Throughout the pattern, finished schoolhouse units will be known as A (spring), B (summer), C (autumn), or D (winter).

1. Referring to **FIGURE 1**, draw a diagonal line on the wrong side of both 1½" (3.8 cm) spring sky squares. Place a marked square on the 1½" × 2½" (3.8 cm × 6.4 cm) spring roof peak rectangle with right sides together, aligning the raw edges. Stitch on the line, then trim and discard the excess fabric. Open the pieced square and press. Repeat on the opposite end of the rectangle to make belfry roof peak A. In the same manner, make belfry roof peaks B, C, and D.

2. Follow the manufacturer's instructions when using the fusible web. Trace 4 of template A on the paper side of the 3" (7.6 cm) fusible web square. Fuse it to the wrong side of the 4" (10.2 cm) gray texture square. Cut the bells out on the drawn lines and set aside.

3. Referring to **FIGURE 2**, sew the ⅞" × 1¾" (2.2 cm × 4.4 cm) spring wall strips to the sides of the 1¾" (4.4 cm) spring sky square. Add the ⅞" × 2½" (2.2 cm × 6.4 cm) spring wall strips to the top and bottom to complete the belfry walled square. Sew belfry roof peak A to the top of the opening, then add the 1½" × 2½" (3.8 cm × 6.4 cm) spring sky rectangle to the top of the peak. Fuse a bell in place at the top of the belfry opening and edgestitch it using a machine blanket or straight stitch and matching thread to complete belfry unit A. In the same manner, make belfry units B-D (**FIGURE 3**). Referring to **FIGURE 4**, sew the 4½" × 7½" (11.4 cm × 19.1 cm) spring sky rectangles to the sides of belfry unit A to complete sky unit A. In the same manner, make sky units B-D (**FIGURE 5**).

4. Trace Templates B, Br (reversed), and C on template plastic, including the seam lines, grain lines, and match points. Cut out the shapes directly on the outer lines, then make small holes at the match points using an awl or large needle. Place the templates on the wrong sides of the appropriate fabrics and mark around the templates. Cut out the fabric shapes and

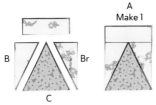

A
Make 1

B C Br

FIGURE 6

B
Make 1

C
Make 1

D
Make 1

FIGURE 7

Roof Unit A
Make 1

FIGURE 8

Roof Unit B
Make 1

Roof Unit C
Make 1

Roof Unit D
Make 1

FIGURE 9

Door Unit A
Make 1

FIGURE 10

Door Unit B
Make 1

Door Unit C
Make 1

Door Unit D
Make 1

FIGURE 11

mark the match points on the wrong side of each. Referring to **FIGURE 6** and aligning the match points, sew spring roof B and Br shapes to the sides of the spring roof peak C shape. Add the 1½" × 3½" (3.8 cm × 8.9 cm) spring roof strip to the top to complete porch roof A. Make porch roofs B-D in the same manner (**FIGURE 7**). Referring to **FIGURE 8**, sew 4½" × 5" (11.4 cm × 12.7 cm) spring roof rectangles to the sides of porch roof A to complete roof unit A. In the same manner, make roof units B-D (**FIGURE 9**).

5. Referring to **FIGURE 10**, sew the 1¼" × 5¾" (3.2 cm × 14.6 cm) spring wall strips to the sides of the 3½" × 5¾" (8.9 cm × 14.6 cm) spring door rectangle. Add the 1¼" × 5" (3.2 cm × 12.7 cm) spring wall strip to the top to complete door unit A. In the same manner, make door units B-D (**FIGURE 11**).

6. Sew the 1⅝" × 5¼" (4.1 cm × 13.3 cm) spring wall strips to the sides of a 2" × 5¼" (5.1 cm × 13.3 cm) spring window strip (**FIGURE 12**). Add a 1¾" × 4¼" (4.4 cm × 10.8 cm) spring wall strip to the bottom to complete window unit A. Make 2. In the same manner, make 2 each of window units B-D (**FIGURE 13**).

Window Unit A
Make 2

FIGURE 12

Window Unit B
Make 2

Window Unit C
Make 2

Window Unit D
Make 2

FIGURE 13

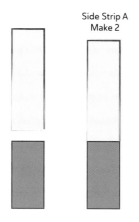

Side Strip A
Make 2

FIGURE 14

7. Referring to **FIGURE 14**, stitch together (1) 2½" × 6½" (6.4 cm × 16.5 cm) spring sky strip and (1) 2½" × 4½" (6.4 cm × 11.4 cm) spring ground strip to make an A side strip. Make 2. In the same manner, make 2 each of B, C, and D side strips (**FIGURE 15**).

8. Note the orientation of the various units throughout block assembly. Referring to the **Schoolhouse Block Assembly Diagram**, sew together 2 window and 1 door units A, alternating. Stitch roof unit A to the top, then add the A side strips to the sides. Sew sky unit A to the top and the 16½" (42 cm) spring ground strip to the bottom to complete the Spring Schoolhouse block. Use the B units to make the Summer Schoolhouse block, the C units to make the Autumn Schoolhouse block, and the D units to make the Winter Schoolhouse block in the same manner.

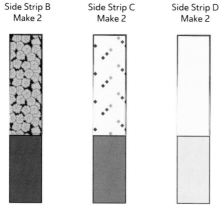

Side Strip B
Make 2

Side Strip C
Make 2

Side Strip D
Make 2

FIGURE 15

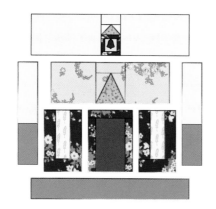

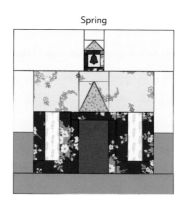

Spring

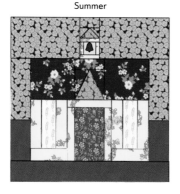

Summer

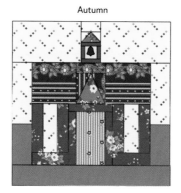

Autumn

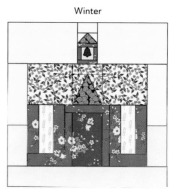

Winter

SCHOOLHOUSE BLOCK ASSEMBLY DIAGRAM

Make 20 each of D and E
and 20 each of F and G

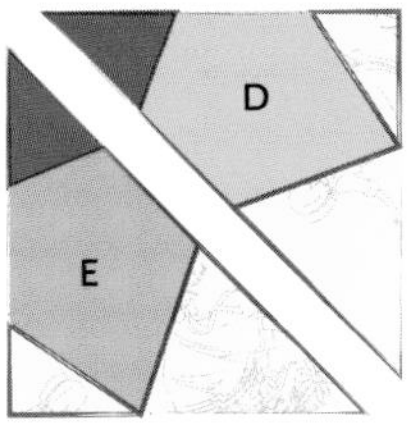

Make 20 D/E
Make 16 F/G

FIGURE 16

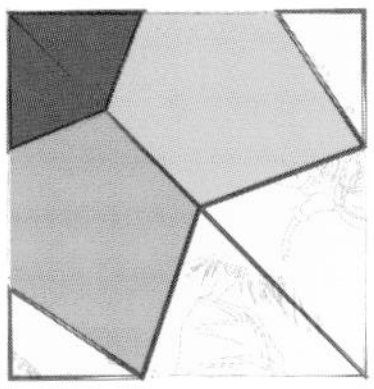

FIGURE 17

Make 5 large sunflowers
and 4 small sunflowers

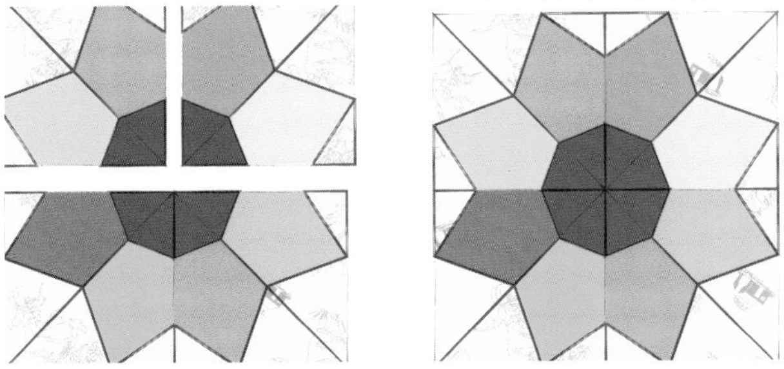

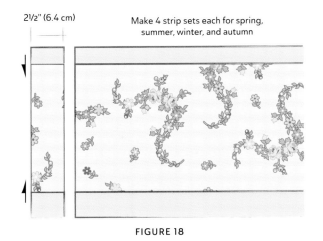

SUNFLOWER BLOCK ASSEMBLY DIAGRAM

2½" (6.4 cm)

Make 4 strip sets each for spring,
summer, winter, and autumn

FIGURE 18

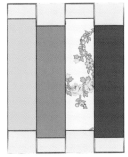

BOOK BLOCK ASSEMBLY DIAGRAM

PIECING THE SUNFLOWER BLOCKS
Finished block size (large): 16" (40.6 cm) square
Finished block size (small): 10" (25.4 cm) square

9. If you need help with foundation paper piecing, refer to Foundation Paper Piecing in Chapter 1. Make 20 accurate copies each of Foundation Masters D and E. Make 16 accurate copies each of Foundation Masters F and G. Referring to the Foundation Masters and Cutting Instructions for patch placement, paper piece 20 total each of D and E (**FIGURE 16**). In the same manner, paper piece 16 total each of F and G (**FIGURE 17**). Referring to the **Sunflower Block Assembly Diagram**, stitch together (4) of D and (4) of E to make 1 large Sunflower block. Make 5 total.

10. In the same manner, stitch together (4) of F and (4) of G to make 1 small Sunflower block. Make 4 total.

PIECING THE BOOK BLOCKS
Finished block size: 8" × 10" (20.3 cm × 25.4 cm)

11. Referring to **FIGURE 18**, stitch together (1) 1½" (3.8 cm) light tan strip, (1) 8" (20.3 cm) spring book strip, and (1) 2" (5.1 cm) light tan strip to make a spring book strip set. Press in the direction of the arrows. Make 4 total. Cut (7) 2½" (6.4 cm) wide segments from each strip set for a total of 28 spring segments. In the same manner, make 4 total each summer, autumn, and winter book strip sets, press, and then cut segments.

12. Sew 4 different spring segments together as shown to make a spring Book block (**Book Block Assembly Diagram**). Make 7. In the same manner, make 7 Book blocks each of summer, autumn, and winter book fabrics.

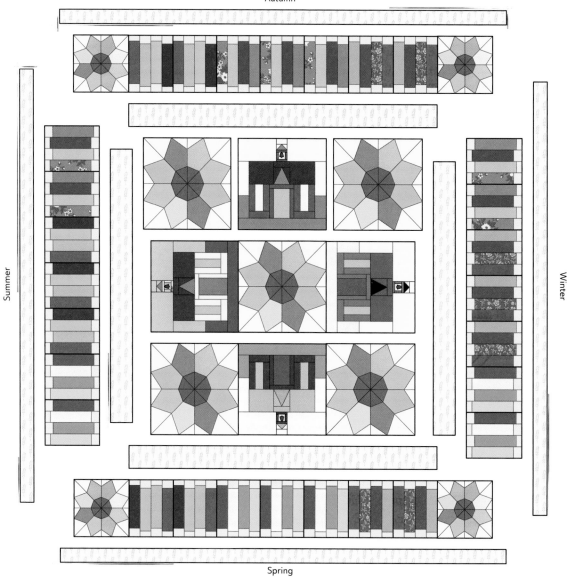

Autumn

Summer

Winter

Spring

ASSEMBLY DIAGRAM

ASSEMBLING THE QUILT TOP

Refer to the **Assembly Diagram** and note block and strip orientations carefully throughout assembly.

13. Sew 3 rows using the Schoolhouse and large Sunflower blocks, making sure that the schoolhouses face toward the center. Stitch the rows together. Sew (1) 48½" (123.2 cm) tan house strips to each side with the printed houses facing toward the center. Stitch the 56½" (143.8 cm) house strips to the top and bottom, again with the printed houses facing in.

14. Each side of the quilt features book blocks from the season of the schoolhouse closest to it, as well as book blocks from the seasons to either side. For

example, to make the book strip for the summer side of the quilt, sew together 2 spring Book blocks, 3 summer Book blocks, and 2 Autumn book blocks, in that order. Sew together 2 winter Book blocks, 3 spring Book blocks, and 2 summer Book blocks to make the book strip for the spring side of the quilt. Use the remaining book blocks to make the autumn and winter book strips in the same manner.

15. Sew the Summer book strip to the Summer side of the quilt and the Winter book strip to the Winter side. Sew a small Sunflower block to each end of the Spring book strip and join to the Spring side of the quilt. Sew a small Sunflower block to each end of the Autumn strip and sew it to the Autumn side.

16. Measure the length of the quilt from raw edge to raw edge through the middle. Trim the 80" (203.2 cm) tan house strips to this measurement and sew to the sides of the quilt.

17. Measure the width of the quilt from raw edge to raw edge through the middle. Trim the 86" (218.4 cm) house strips to this measurement and sew to the top and bottom of the quilt.

FINISHING
18. Sew the 11" (27.9 cm) backing strips together end-to-end to make the center strip of the backing. Stitch a 90½" (229.9 cm) backing strip to either side of the pieced strip to complete the backing. Layer the backing (wrong-side up), the batting, and the quilt top (right-side up), and baste them together.

19. Quilt as desired, then bind.

BEADS FOR CARRIE

For me, one of the most memorable stories in *Little House on the Prairie* is when Pa takes Mary and Laura to the abandoned Indian camp and they find beads in the dust. They search all afternoon until each girl has a handful of beads. When they get home, the sisters string the beads on thread to make a beautiful necklace for Carrie.

This quilt is just the right size for a preschooler like Carrie. The appliquéd beads represent the beads in the dust, while the pieced border represents the beads strung on thread. Feel free to put as many, or as few, beads in your quilt center as you wish. I've used the colors mentioned in the book, but your beads can be almost any color and still be historically accurate. The Plains Indians traded with tribes in the Pacific Northwest, in Minnesota, and even along the Gulf of Mexico. Because of their wide trading range, they were able to make beads from colorful shells, mineral-rich soil, such as brown catlinite and white caliche, and even from bone. The beads in this quilt are modeled after the glass beads that the Europeans began trading with the Indians in the 1850s. They were uniformly round, brightly colored, and were the most popular type of beads in the Kansas Territory when the Ingalls family was there.

MATERIALS

2⅛ yards (1.9 m) tan girl print for the quilt center and pieced border

⅜ yard (0.3 m) gray floral for the "thread" strip in the pieced border

1½ yards (1.4 m) total assorted blue, red, green, brown, and white florals, prints, and textures for the appliqué and pieced border

⅝ yard (0.6 m) green floral for the outer border

3⅛ yards (2.9 m) backing fabric

½ yard (0.5 m) blue floral for the binding

51" × 63" (129.5 cm × 160 cm) batting

1½ yards (1.4 m) paper-backed fusible web (at least 17" [43.2 cm] wide) for the appliqué

See-through template plastic

Trimming template (see Chapter 3)

Templates A, B, and C (see Chapter 3)

Finished size: 43" × 55" (109.2 cm × 139.7 cm)
Pieced and appliquéd by Katie Melich
Quilted by Donna Smith

CUTTING INSTRUCTIONS

For best use of fabric, cut patches in the order listed. The templates for the beads are printed without turn-under allowances to use with paper-backed fusible web. There are three sizes of beads, which all share the same size cut-out circle for the hole. If you wish to hand-appliqué your beads, remember to add turn-under allowances. **Note**: Border strips include extra length for trimming.

From the tan girl print, cut:
(1) 26" × 38" (66 cm × 96.5 cm) rectangle
(6) 3¾" (9.5 cm) × WOF (width-of-fabric) strips
(4) 7¼" (18.4 cm) squares
(4) 3¾" (9.5 cm) squares
(26) 1¾" × 2" (4.4 cm × 5.1 cm) rectangles
(26) 1⅛" × 2" (2.9 cm × 5.1 cm) rectangles
(160) 1¼" (3.2 cm) squares

From the gray floral, cut:
(3) ¾" (1.9 cm) × WOF strips
(4) 4" (10.2 cm) squares

From the assorted blue, red, green, brown, and white florals, prints, and textures, cut a total of:
(14) 2" × 7¼" (5.1 cm × 18.4 cm) strips
(13) 2" × 6" (5.1 cm × 15.2 cm) strips
(13) 2" × 4¾" (5.1 cm × 12.1 cm) strips
(20) Template A
(6) Template B
(6) Template C

From the green floral, cut:
(2) 3" × 54" (7.6 cm × 137.2 cm) strips for the borders, pieced from 3 WOF strips
(2) 3" × 46" (7.6 cm × 116.8 cm) strips for the borders, pieced from 3 WOF strips

From the blue floral, cut:
(6) 2¼" (5.7 cm) × WOF strips for the binding

APPLIQUÉING THE BEADS

Note: The 26" × 38" (66 cm × 96.5 cm) tan rectangle is cut oversized to allow for shrinkage during appliqué. It will be trimmed in step 2.

1. Trace (21) A Templates, (6) B Templates, and (6) C Templates (including the center circle on each) on the paper side of the fusible web. Cut the templates apart, leaving a small margin beyond the drawn lines. Fuse the templates to the wrong side of the appropriate fabrics and cut them out on the drawn lines. Cut out and discard the center circles (see the Half-Pint Tip Appliqué without Stiffness in Braids, Bonnets, and Bows).

2. Referring to the quilt photo for bead placement, finger press the 26" × 38" (66 cm × 96.5 cm) tan rectangle in half lengthwise and widthwise. Using the folds as a guide, position the beads on the tan rectangle as you wish, keeping in mind that the rectangle will be trimmed at the end of this step. Fuse the beads in place. Edgestitch the appliqué using a machine straight or decorative stitch of your choice, in either matching thread or monofilament (see Edgestitching Appliqué in Chapter 1). Centering the appliqué, trim the rectangle to 24½" × 36½" (62.2 cm × 92.7 cm).

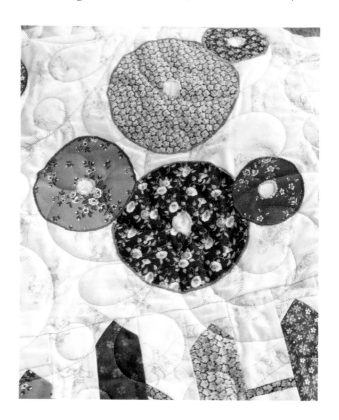

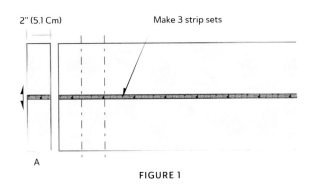

FIGURE 1

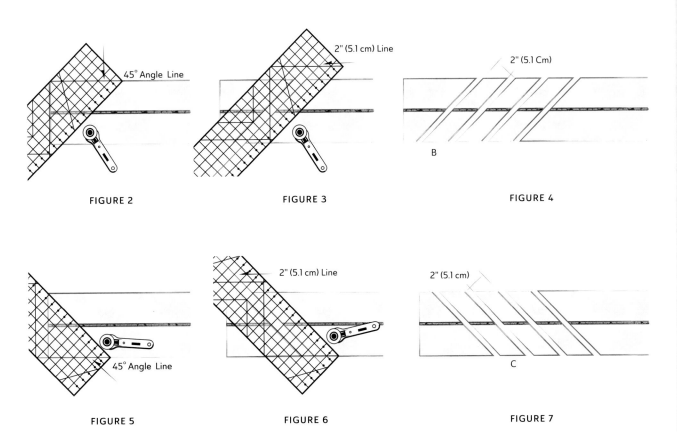

FIGURE 2

FIGURE 3

FIGURE 4

FIGURE 5

FIGURE 6

FIGURE 7

MAKING THE PIECED BORDER

3. Referring to **FIGURE 1**, sew together (2) 3¾" (9.5 cm) tan strips and (1) ¾" (1.9 cm) gray strip to make a strip set. Press seam allowances in the direction of the arrows. Make 3 strip sets. Cut 1 strip set into (20) 2" (5.1 cm) wide A segments.

4. Referring to **FIGURE 2**, align the 45° angle line of a rotary cutting ruler with the upper edge of 1 of the remaining strip sets. Trim the end. Referring to

FIGURE 3 and **4**, cut (10) 2" (5.1 cm) wide B segments. In a similar manner, align the 45° angle line of the ruler with the bottom edge of the remaining strip set (**FIGURE 5**). Trim the end, then cut (10) 2" (5.1 cm) wide C segments (**FIGURES 6** and **7**).

5. Trace the Trimming Template onto the template plastic, including the seam lines. Cut it out on the outer marked line. Position the Trimming Template right-side up on a B segment, aligning the drawn seam

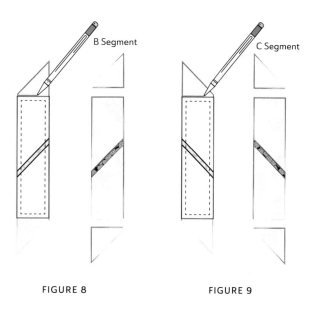

B Segment

C Segment

FIGURE 8

FIGURE 9

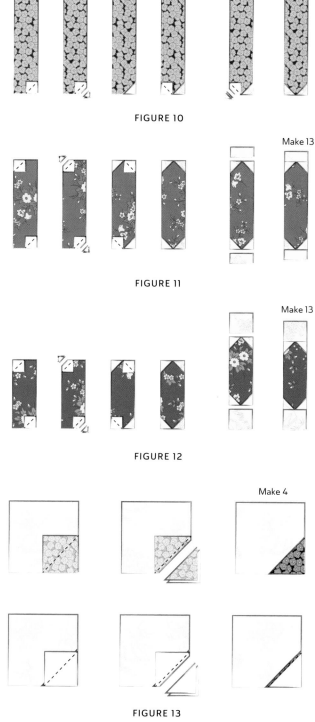

Make 14

FIGURE 10

Make 13

FIGURE 11

Make 13

FIGURE 12

Make 4

FIGURE 13

lines with the seam lines of the segment (**FIGURE 8**). Draw lines along the top and bottom edges of the template. Cutting directly on the lines, trim the excess fabric to complete a B segment. In the same manner, trim the remaining B segments. With the Trimming Template right-side down on the C segments, trim them in the same manner (**FIGURE 9**).

6. Draw a diagonal line on the wrong side of each 1¼" (3.2 cm) tan square. Referring to **FIGURE 10**, place a marked square on a 2" × 7¼" (5.1 cm × 18.4 cm) assorted strip, right sides together and edges aligned. Stitch on the drawn line. Trim the excess fabric, then open and press. Repeat on the remaining corners of the strip to make 1 long pieced bead. Make 14 total.

In the same manner, sew 1¼" (3.2 cm) tan squares to the corners of a 2" × 6" (5.1 cm × 15.2 cm) assorted strip (**FIGURE 11**). Add 1⅛" × 2" (2.9 cm × 5.1 cm) tan rectangles to the ends to make 1 medium pieced bead. Make 13 total.

Referring to **FIGURE 12**, sew 1¼" (3.2 cm) tan squares to the corners of an assorted 2" × 4¾" (5.1 cm × 12.1 cm) strip, then add 1¾" × 2" (4.4 cm × 5.1 cm) tan rectangles to each end to make 1 short pieced bead. Make 13 total.

7. Draw a diagonal line on the wrong side of each 4" (10.2 cm) gray square. Referring to **FIGURE 13**, place a marked square on a 7¼" (18.4 cm) tan square, right sides together and edges aligned. Stitch on the drawn line. Trim the excess fabric, then open and press to

make a pieced square. Draw a diagonal line on the wrong side of each 3¾" (9.5 cm) tan square. Place a marked tan square on the gray corner of the pieced square, right sides together and edges aligned. Sew on the drawn line. Trim the excess fabric, then open and press to complete 1 corner square. Make 4.

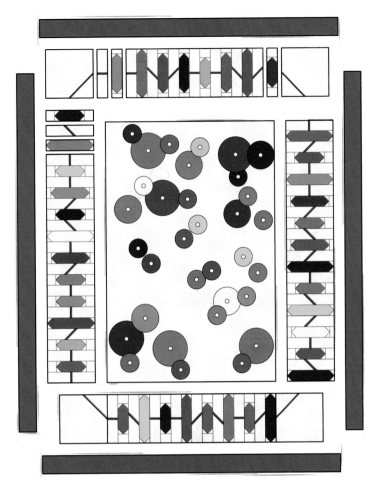

ASSEMBLY DIAGRAM

ASSEMBLING THE QUILT TOP

Refer to the **Assembly Diagram** throughout assembly.

8. Starting with an A segment, sew together 12 total segments and 12 total pieced beads, alternating, to make a side border strip. Repeat to make a second side border strip, then sew a strip to either side of the quilt center. Starting with an A segment each time, make top and bottom border strips using 8 total segments and 8 total pieced beads each, alternating. Noting the orientation, sew corner squares to the ends of the top and bottom border strips. Stitch the border strips to the top and bottom of the quilt, so that corner square 'threads' align with border strip 'threads.'

9. Measure the length of the quilt through the middle from raw edge to raw edge. Trim the 54" (137.2 cm)

green floral strips to this length and sew them to the sides of the quilt. Measure the width of the quilt through the middle from raw edge to raw edge. Trim the 46" (116.8 cm) green floral strips to this length and sew them to the top and bottom of the quilt.

FINISHING

10. Piece the quilt backing widthwise, making sure it is at least 8" (20.3 cm) longer and wider than the quilt top. Layer the backing (wrong-side up), the batting, and the quilt top (right-side up), and baste them together.

11. Quilt as desired, and then bind the quilt with the blue floral strips.

GENTLE GRACE
CRADLE QUILT

This classic design was a favorite in the latter half of the nineteenth century. Easily pieced and a perfect pattern for using up scraps, it made a good first project for a beginning quilter. The same is true today. While the pattern calls for lengths of fabrics, this quilt can also be made completely from scraps. Just cut 1½" (3.8 cm) squares instead of 1½" (3.8 cm) strips, then sew the Four-Patches blocks from squares.

This quilt was also popular with young girls and their mothers because the many squares provide an easy-to-follow grid for quilting.

MATERIALS

¼ yard (0.2 m) each pink small floral, green small floral, and gold small floral for the Four-Patch blocks

5/8 yard (0.3 m) turquoise small floral for the blocks and binding

7/8 yard (0.8 m) total of assorted light tan prints for the blocks

1¼ yards (1.1 m) light pink floral for the setting squares and outer border

¼ yard (0.2 m) tan prairie print for the inner border

15/8 yards (1.5 m) backing fabric

39" × 50" (99.1 cm × 127 cm) batting

Finished size: 31" × 42½" (78.7 cm × 108 cm)
Pieced by Rae Strauss and Laura Stone Roberts
Quilted by Donna Smith

CUTTING INSTRUCTIONS

For best use of fabric, cut the strips and patches in the order listed. **Note**: Border strips include extra length for trimming.

From the pink small floral, green small floral, and gold small floral, cut a total of:
(7) 1½" (3.8 cm) × WOF (width-of-fabric) strips

From the turquoise small floral, cut:
(3) 1½" (3.8 cm) × WOF strips
(4) 2¼" (5.7 cm) x WOF strips for the binding

From the light tan prints, cut a total of:
(10) 1½" (3.8 cm) × WOF strips

From the light pink floral, cut:
(2) 1¾" (4.4 cm) × WOF strips for outer borders
(2) 1¾" × 34" (4.4 cm × 86.4 cm) strips for outer borders
(124) 2½" (6.4 cm) squares

From the tan prairie print, cut:
(2) 1¼" (3.2 cm) × WOF strips for inner borders
(2) 1¼" × 32" (3.2 cm × 81.3 cm) strips for inner borders

From the backing fabric, cut:
(1) 39" × 50" (99.1 cm × 127 cm) rectangle

PIECING THE FOUR-PATCH BLOCKS
Finished block size: 2" (5.1 cm) square

1. Referring to **FIGURE 1**, sew together (1) 1½" (3.8 cm) light tan strip and (1) 1½" (3.8 cm) pink, green, gold, or turquoise strip to make a strip set. Make 10 strip sets total, pressing in the direction of the arrow. Cut the strip sets into a total of (246) 1½" (3.8 cm) wide segments.

2. Referring to **FIGURE 2**, stitch 2 segments together to make a Four-Patch block. Make 123 Four-Patch blocks total.

ASSEMBLING THE QUILT TOP
Refer to the **Assembly Diagram**.

3. Noting the orientation of the Four-Patch blocks, sew together (7) 2½" (6.4 cm) light pink squares and 6 Four-Patch blocks, alternating, to make an odd-numbered row. Make 10.

4. Sew together 7 Four-Patch blocks and (6) 2½" (6.4 cm) light pink squares, alternating, to make an even-numbered row. Make 9.

5. Stitch the odd- and even-numbered rows together alternately to make the quilt center.

1½" (3.8 cm)

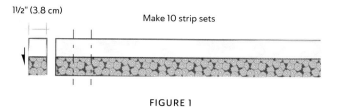

Make 10 strip sets

FIGURE 1

Make 123

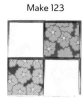

FIGURE 2

Four-Patch Block

ASSEMBLY DIAGRAM

6. Measure the length of the quilt through the middle from raw edge to raw edge. Trim both of the 1¼" (3.2 cm) × WOF tan prairie print strips to this measurement and sew them to the sides of the quilt. In the same manner, measure the width of the quilt. Trim the 1¼" × 32" (3.2 cm × 81.3 cm) tan prairie print strips to this measurement. Sew them to the top and bottom of the quilt.

7. In the same manner, measure the quilt length. Trim the 1¾" (4.4 cm) × WOF light pink strips to match this measurement, then sew them to the sides of the quilt. Repeat, measuring the quilt width, and trimming and sewing the top/bottom borders with the

remaining 1¾" (4.4 cm) strips. Sew them to the top and bottom of the quilt.

FINISHING
8. Layer the backing (wrong-side up), the batting, and the quilt top (right-side up), and baste them together.

9. Quilt as desired, then bind the quilt with the turquoise floral.

PRAIRIE BLOOMS TABLE RUNNER

Can you imagine eating your lunch in the middle of a prairie with grasses waving in the wind around you and the bluest of blue skies above? If you were Laura Ingalls, you'd be sitting on that grass with your plate on your lap, admiring the tin cup of pretty flowers on the wagon step. Sadly, my kitchen looks nothing like a richly beautiful prairie. And my table isn't nearly as romantic as a wagon step. But with this table runner, I can have flowers on my table even when the snow is falling and the ground is frozen solid.

You'll be surprised at how quickly this table runner comes together. Simple Four-Patch blocks and fusible-web appliqué make this the perfect project for a snowy or rainy day. These fabric colors make me think of autumn suppers and fall leaves, but you can easily make this a springtime decoration by substituting fresh yellows, greens, pinks, and white for the fabrics listed.

MATERIALS

10" (25.4 cm) square each of tan prairie print, brown vine print, tan girl print, brown bouquet print, gray vine floral, and gray small floral

3/8 yard (0.3 m) tan/gray/gold mini-dot for the pieced setting triangles and corner triangles

7/8 yard (0.8 m) gray bouquet print for the pieced setting triangles, border, and binding

1/8 yard (0.1 m) each of red bouquet print, gold narrow stripe, red vine print, and tan-and-brown leaf print for the flowers

1 3/4 yards (1.6 m) backing fabric

23" × 59" (58.4 cm × 150 cm) batting

1 1/4 yards (1.1 m) paper-backed fusible web (at least 17" [43.2 cm] wide) for the appliqué

See-through template plastic

Appliqué pressing sheet

Flower template (see Chapter 3)

Finished size: 16½" × 52½" (41.9 cm × 133.4 cm)
Pieced and appliquéd by Rae Strauss
Quilted by Donna Smith

CUTTING INSTRUCTIONS

For best use of fabric, cut the patches below in the order they're listed. The flower template is printed without turn-under allowance to use with paper-backed fusible web. If you wish to hand-appliqué your blooms, remember to add a turn-under allowance to the flower shape. **Note**: Border strips include extra length for trimming.

From each of the tan prairie, brown vine, tan girl print, and brown bouquet prints, cut:
(4) 4¾" (12.1 cm) squares

From both the gray vine and gray small floral, cut:
(2) 4¾" (12.1 cm) squares

From the tan/gray/gold mini-dot, cut:
(3) 7¼" (18.4 cm) squares; cut each in half twice diagonally to make 12 quarter-square triangles
(2) 8" (20.3 cm) squares; cut each in half diagonally to make 4 half-square triangles

From the gray bouquet print, cut:
(4) 2¼" (5.7 cm) × WOF (width-of-fabric) strips for the binding
(2) 2½" × 52" (6.4 cm × 132.1 cm) strips, pieced from 3 WOF strips
(2) 2½" × 20" (6.4 cm × 50.8 cm) strips
(2) 4¾" (12.1 cm) squares

From both the red bouquet print and the gold narrow stripe, cut:
(1) 3½" × 32" (8.9 cm × 81.3 cm) strip

From both the red vine print and the tan/brown leaf print, cut:
(1) 3½" × 26" (8.9 cm × 66 cm) strip

From the backing fabric, cut:
(1) 23" × 59" (58.4 cm × 150 cm) strip

MAKING BLOCKS AND SETTING TRIANGLES
Finished Bloom block size: 8½" (21.6 cm) square

1. Referring to FIGURE 1, sew together (2) 4¾" (12.1 cm) brown vine squares and (2) 4¾" (12.1 cm) tan prairie squares to make 1 Four-Patch block A. Make 2 blocks. In the same manner, use the 4¾" (12.1 cm) brown bouquet and tan girl print squares to make 2 of Four-Patch block B.

2. Referring to FIGURE 2, sew (2) 7¼" (18.4 cm) mini-dot triangles to a 4¾" (12.1 cm) gray vine square to create 1 setting triangle C. Make 2. In the same manner, stitch (2) 7¼" (18.4 cm) mini-dot triangles to each of the 4¾" (12.1 cm) gray bouquet squares to make 2 setting triangles D, then sew (2) 7¼" (18.4 cm) mini-dot triangles to each of the 4¾" (12.1 cm) gray small floral squares to make 2 setting triangles E.

3. Referring to FIGURE 3, sew together the 3½" (8.9 cm) gold stripe and the red bouquet strips to make a strip set. Press in the direction of the arrow, then cut the strip set into (8) 3½" (8.9 cm) segments. In the same manner, make a strip set with the 3½" (8.9 cm) red vine and the tan/brown print strips (FIGURE 4). Cut the strip set into (6) 3½" (8.9 cm) wide segments.

4. Referring to FIGURE 5, sew 2 matching segments together to make a small Four-Patch unit. Make in the quantities shown.

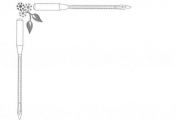

HALF-PINT TIP
Use New Needles

Change the needle in your sewing machine with every new project. And if you start hearing the needle "pop" when it enters the fabric, change it immediately.

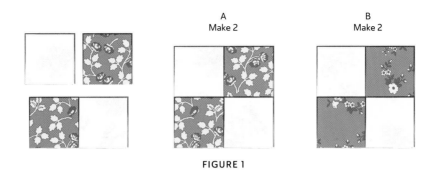

A
Make 2

B
Make 2

FIGURE 1

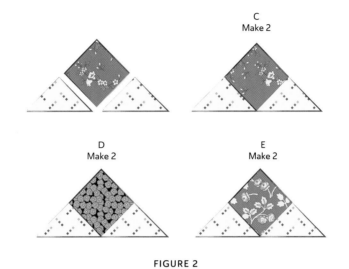

C
Make 2

D
Make 2

E
Make 2

FIGURE 2

3½" (8.9 cm)

Make 1 strip set

3½" (8.9 cm)

Make 1 strip set

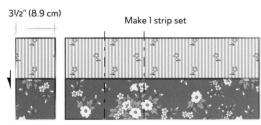

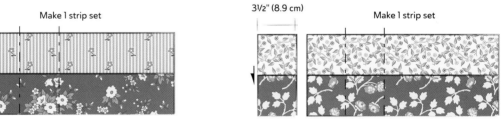

FIGURE 3

FIGURE 4

Make 4

Make 3

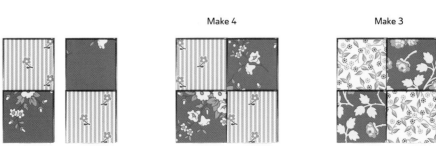

FIGURE 5

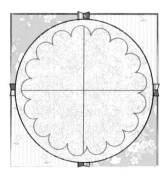

FIGURE 6

F
Make 4

G
Make 3

FIGURE 7

Bloom Block A

Bloom Block B

FIGURE 8

5. Trace the flower template, including the outer circle and the crossing lines, on the paper side of the fusible web 7 times. Cut out on the outer circle. Referring to **FIGURE 6**, position the fusible web template on the wrong side of a small red bouquet/gold stripe Four-Patch unit, aligning the crossing lines on the template with the seam lines of the Four-Patch. Following the manufacturer's instructions, fuse it in place. Cut the flower out to complete (1) F flower. Repeat with the remaining traced templates and small red vine and tan/brown Four-Patch units to make a total of (4) F flowers and (3) G flowers (**FIGURE 7**).

6. Referring to **FIGURE 8**, position (1) F flower on a Four-Patch block from step 1 so that the red quarter-flowers are atop the tan squares and the gold stripe quarter-flowers are atop the brown squares. Aligning seam lines, fuse the flower in place. Edgestitch the flower using a machine straight or decorative stitch of your choice, in either matching thread or mono-filament (see Edgestitching Appliqué in Chapter 1) to complete Bloom block. Repeat with the remaining Four-Patch blocks A and B to make a total of 4 Bloom blocks. **Note:** The G flowers will be used in step 8.

ASSEMBLING THE TABLE RUNNER

7. Referring to the **Assembly Diagram**, sew 4 diagonal rows using the blocks and the setting triangles. Notice that the matching gray squares are positioned opposite each another, with the gray bouquet squares in the center. Sew the rows together. Add the mini-dot 8" (20.3 cm) half-square triangles to the corners and evenly trim them ¼" (6 mm) outside the block corners.

8. Using the same technique as before, fuse and edge-stitch the G flowers in place as shown in **FIGURE 9**, noting the orientation of the flowers and aligning the seams.

9. Measure the length of the table runner down the middle from raw edge to raw edge. Trim the 52" (132.1 cm) gray bouquet strips to this measurement and sew 1 to each side. Measure the width of the table runner in 3 places, from raw edge to raw edge. Add the 3 measurements together and divide by 3 to get the

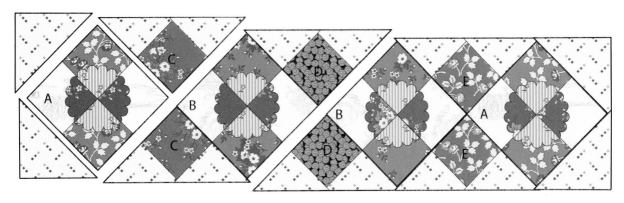

ASSEMBLY DIAGRAM

FIGURE 9

average width. Trim the 20" (50.8 cm) gray bouquet strips to this measurement and sew them to the ends.

FINISHING THE TABLE RUNNER

10. Layer the backing (wrong-side up), the batting, and the table runner top (right-side up), and baste them together.

11. Quilt as desired, then bind the table runner with the gray bouquet 2¼" (5.7 cm) strips.

CROW PLACEMATS AND NAPKINS

There are many birds in the *Little House* books. Geese, ducks, blackbirds, prairie hens, and crows are all a part of Laura's world. I like the crows the best. In *Little House on the Prairie,* there's a scene describing a midsummer moment with cawing crows suddenly flying overhead. I can just hear them now!

Considered as being among the most intelligent of birds, crows have a complex language and incredible memorization abilities, and they can even use tools. If a member of the flock is injured, other crows will care for it until it is well or grieve for it when it dies. Crows are also farmers' friends. While crows have long been considered pests for eating crops, a nestling can eat 100 grasshoppers in just three hours. And with this placemat and napkin set, you can eat with the crows, though I recommend leaving the grasshoppers to them.

MATERIALS

1 fat quarter (18" × 21" (45.7 cm × 53.3 cm]) black texture fabric for the crows

1⅛ yards (1 m) cream wheat print for backgrounds and checkerboards

3½ yards (3.2 m) black/pink floral for the checkerboards, place mat backings, bindings, and napkins

2⅜ yards (2.2 m) tan/black floral for the borders and napkins

44" × 54" (111.8 cm × 137.2 cm) batting for place mats

3/4 yard (0.7 m) paper-backed fusible web (at least 17" [43.2 cm] wide) for the appliqué

(4) ¼–3/8" (6 mm–1 cm) black or silver buttons for eyes

Crow templates (see Chapter 3)

Makes (4) 15½" × 20½" (39.4 cm × 52.1 cm) placemats and (4) 18" (45.7 cm) square napkins
Made by Rae Strauss

CUTTING INSTRUCTIONS

For best use of fabric, cut the patches in the order listed. The template for the crow is printed reversed and without a turn-under allowance to use with paper-backed fusible web. If you wish to hand-appliqué the crows, remember to add turn-under allowances.

From the black texture fabric, cut:
4 crow shapes (see step 1 before cutting)

From the cream wheat print, cut:
(8) 1½" (3.8 cm) × WOF (width-of-fabric) strips
(4) 11" × 14" (27.9 cm × 35.6 cm) rectangles on the crosswise grain
(8) 1½" (3.8 cm) squares

From the black/pink floral, cut:
(8) 2¼" (5.7 cm) × WOF for the bindings
(4) 21" × 26" (53.3 cm × 66 cm) rectangles
(8) 1½" (3.8 cm) × WOF strips
(4) 14½" (36.8 cm) squares
(8) 1½" (3.8 cm) squares

From the tan/black floral, cut:
(4) 18½" (47 cm) squares
(8) 2½" × 20½" (6.4 cm × 52.1 cm) strips
(8) 2½" × 18½" (6.4 cm × 47 cm) strips
(8) 2½" × 14½" (6.4 cm × 36.8 cm) strips
(8) 2½" × 11½" (6.4 cm × 29.2 cm) strips

From the batting, cut:
(4) 21" × 26" (53.3 cm × 66 cm) rectangles

HALF-PINT TIP
Feathering Your Nest

In the spring and fall, take small fabric and batting scraps that you don't want and tuck them into a tree or just under the edge of a rock. Birds and small animals will delight in the comfort you've just added to their nests.

Make 4   Trim line

Fold line

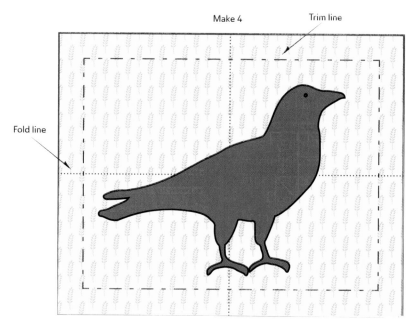

FIGURE 1

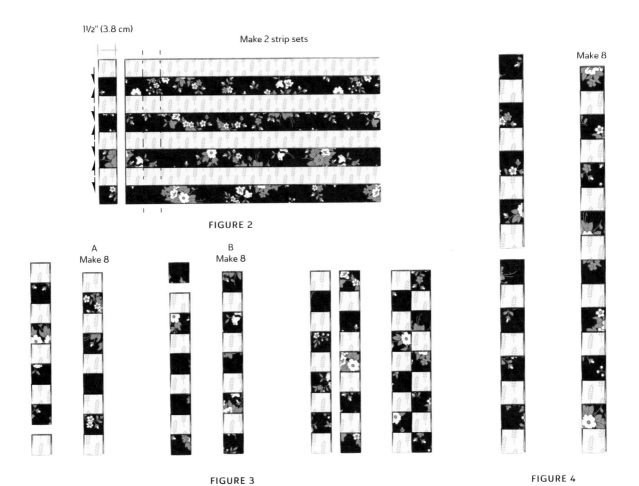

1½" (3.8 cm)

Make 2 strip sets

Make 8

FIGURE 2

A
Make 8

B
Make 8

FIGURE 3

FIGURE 4

APPLIQUÉING THE CROWS

Follow the manufacturer's instructions for using the paper-backed fusible web throughout. **Note**: The 11" × 14" (28.2 cm × 35.6 cm) cream wheat print rectangles are cut oversized to allow for shrinkage during appliqué. They will be trimmed in step 2.

1. Trace 4 crow templates on the paper side of the fusible web. Cut the templates apart, leaving a small margin beyond the drawn lines. Fuse the templates to the wrong side of the black texture, then cut them out on the drawn lines.

2. Finger press each 11" × 14" (28.2 cm × 35.6 cm) cream wheat rectangle in half lengthwise and widthwise. Referring to **FIGURE 1** and using the folds as a guide, center the crow shape on each cream wheat rectangle. Fuse the shape in place, then edgestitch the crow using a machine straight or decorative stitch of your choice in either matching thread or

monofilament (see Edgestitching Appliqué in Chapter 1). Centering the appliqué, trim the rectangles to 9½" × 12½" (24.1 cm × 31.8 cm).

MAKING THE PLACE MATS

3. Referring to **FIGURE 2**, stitch together (4) 1½" (3.8 cm) × WOF cream wheat strips and (4) 1½"(3.8 cm) × WOF black/pink strips, alternating, to make a strip set. Make 2 strip sets, pressing in the direction of the arrows. Cut the strip sets into (32) 1½" (3.8 cm) wide segments.

4. Referring to **FIGURE 3**, sew a 1½" (3.8 cm) cream square to the bottom of a segment to make (1) A segment. Make 8. Sew a 1½" (3.8 cm) black/pink floral square to the top of a segment to make (1) B segment. Make 8. Stitch (1) A segment and (1) B segment together to make 1 side unit. Make 8. Sew 2 original segments together, end to end and alternating colors, to make 1 pieced strip (**FIGURE 4**). Make 8.

ASSEMBLY DIAGRAM

Make 4

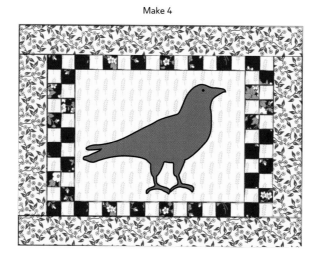

5. Refer to the **Assembly Diagram** and note the orientation of the fabric throughout assembly. Stitch a side unit to either side of an appliquéd rectangle, then sew pieced strips to the top and bottom. Sew (1) 2½" × 11½" (6.4 cm × 29.2 cm) tan/black floral strip to either side, then (1) 2½" × 20½" (6.4 cm × 52.1 cm) tan/black floral strip to the top and 1 to the bottom to complete the placemat top. Make 4.

6. Layer the placemat top with the batting and the 21" × 26" (53.3 cm × 66 cm) black/pink floral rectangles, then baste and quilt. (Tan thread was used to quilt in the ditch between the center rectangle and the checkerboards as well as between the checkerboards and the tan/black floral border.) Trim the backing and batting even with the placemat top, and then bind the placemats with the 2¼" (5.7 cm) black/pink floral strips. Sew the buttons in place for the eyes.

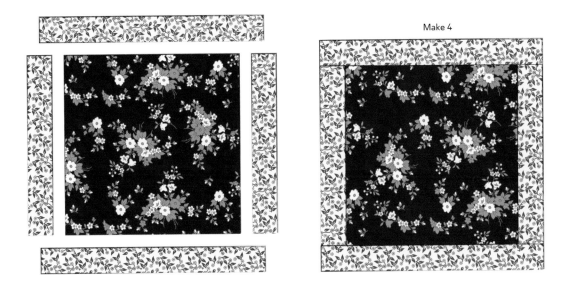

Make 4

FIGURE 5

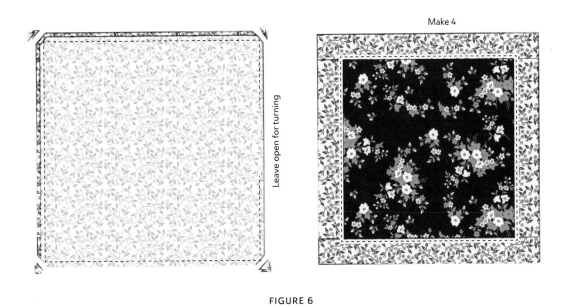

Leave open for turning

Make 4

FIGURE 6

MAKING THE NAPKINS

7. Referring to **FIGURE 5**, stitch 14½" (36.8 cm) tan/black floral strips to the sides of a 14½" (36.8 cm) black/pink floral square. Sew 18½" (47 cm) tan/black floral strips to the top and bottom to complete the napkin front. Make 4.

8. Layer a napkin front and a 18½" (47 cm) tan/black floral square, right sides together (**FIGURE 6**). Sew a ¼" (6 mm) seam around the napkin, leaving an opening for turning on 1 side. Trim the corners, then turn the napkin right side out and press. Handstitch the opening closed. Sewing through both layers, stitch in the ditch around the center square. Repeat to make 4.

THREE SISTERS APRON

Pioneer women and girls often wore aprons over their dresses to protect them from getting dirty or torn. This half apron is perfect for practicing piecing and block-making skills. It makes up in an afternoon and lets you play with lots of coordinating fabric prints. No time for piecing? Make the apron without the blocks by creating the pocket panel from two pieces cut the size of the pocket lining.

MATERIALS

½ yard (0.5 m) yellow daisy stripe
⅞ yard (0.8 m) gray floral vine print
(12) 5" (12.7 cm) squares assorted fabrics for the quilt blocks
Removable marking pen
Block templates (see Chapter 3)

Finished size: 20¾" × 26½" (52.7 cm × 67.3 cm) wide (excluding ties)
Made and written by Amelia Johanson

CUTTING INSTRUCTIONS

From the yellow daisy stripe, cut:

(2) 2½" × 27½" (6.4 cm × 69.9 cm) sashing strips, on the crosswise grain

(3) 2½" × 4½" (6.4 cm × 11.4 cm) sashing strips, on the lengthwise grain

(2) 3" × 4½" (7.5 cm × 11.4 cm) sashing strips, on the lengthwise grain

(1) 8½" × 27¾" (21.6 cm × 70.5 cm) panel for pocket backing

From the gray floral vine, cut:

(1) 23½" × 27½" (59.7 cm × 69.9 cm) panel for apron base

(1) 2½"× 60" (6.4 cm × 152.4 cm) strip for tie (piece as needed)

HALF-PINT TIP
Designing Blocks

Designing blocks is easier than you might think. To end up with a finished 4" (10.2 cm) block like on this apron, draw a 4½" (11.4 cm) square on paper. Using a pencil and straight edge, draw geometric shapes within the square. Copy your design onto heavier paper, such as card stock, then cut out the pieces, adding an exact ¼" (6 mm) seam allowance on each cut edge of the individual pieces. Trace the pieces onto fabric, cut, and reassemble them, following the block design.

CUTTING AND PIECING THE BLOCKS
Finished size: 4" (10.2 cm)

Cut and piece the 4 blocks from the 5" (12.7 cm) squares. Press all seams toward the darker fabric. See Chapter 1 for tips on cutting triangles and the Half-Pint Tip in My Peace of the Prairie for sewing triangles together.

1. Cut (1) 3" (7.6 cm) square from each of (2) 5" (12.7 cm) squares, then cut the squares in half once diagonally to create 4 half-square triangles. Sew the half-square triangles together as shown, squaring up the units to 2½" (6.4 cm). Referring to **FIGURE 1**, join the 4 units together as shown to make 1 Pinwheel block.

2. Cut (2) A triangles from the first fabric, and (1) A triangle and (1) B piece each from second and third fabrics. Referring to **FIGURE 2**, join the pieces together as shown.

3. Cut (2) C triangles from the first fabric, (2) C triangles from a second fabric, (2) D triangles from a third fabric, and (2) 2½" (6.4 cm) squares from a fourth fabric. Referring to **FIGURE 3**, join the pieces together as shown.

4. Cut (1) 1⅜" × 2¾" (3.5 cm × 7 cm) E rectangle and (1) 1⅜" × 3⅝" (3.5 cm × 9.2 cm) F rectangle from the first fabric, (1) 3⅝" (9.2 cm) square from a second fabric, and (2) 1⅜" (3.5 cm) squares from a third fabric. Referring to **FIGURE 4**, join the pieces together as shown.

5. Using a ruler or 4½" (11.4 cm) template, square up each block, trimming the edges evenly.

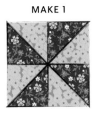

MAKE 1

Pinwheel Block
Block 1

FIGURE 1

A   A   A   A

B

B

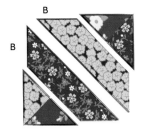
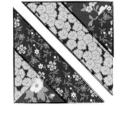

MAKE 1

Block 2

FIGURE 2

C   C   C   C

D

D

MAKE 1

Block 3

FIGURE 3

F

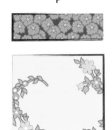
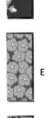

E

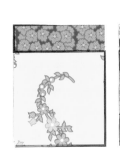
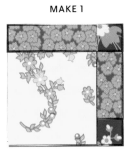

MAKE 1

Block 4

FIGURE 4

FIGURE 5

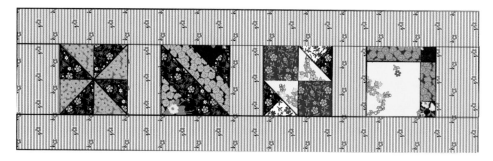

FIGURE 6

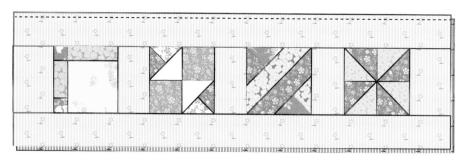

FIGURE 7

MAKING THE BLOCK PANEL

6. Following **FIGURE 5** and using a ¼" (6 mm) seam allowance, join the blocks with the sashing strips. Note that the 3" (7.5 cm) sashing strips are on each end and the 2½" (6.4 cm) strips are between the blocks. Press all seams toward the sashing.

7. Stitch the 2½" × 27½" (6.4 cm × 69.9 cm) sashing strips to the top and bottom of the pieced block panel (**FIGURE 6**) and press.

8. With the right sides together, place the finished block panel on top of the 8½" × 27½" (21.6 cm × 69.9 cm) daisy stripe panel. Stitch across the top with a ¼" (6 mm) seam (**FIGURE 7**). Press the seam open, then fold the quilt block strip to the right side and press along the seam creating the lined pocket piece. Baste across the bottom and pin along the sides.

9. With the right side of the pocket piece facing the wrong side of the apron, align the bottom of the pocket piece with the bottom of the apron. Stitch across the bottom with a ¼" (6 mm) seam. Press the seam open, then fold the pocket piece to the right side of the apron and press. Baste the sides of the pocket to the apron.

10. Referring to **FIGURE 8**, pin the pocket to the front of the apron along the top vertical sashing strips. Using a removable marking pen and a straight edge ruler, draw a straight line down the center of the 3 middle sashing strips. Using matching thread, sew along the drawn lines from the apron hem to the pocket top, reinforcing stitching at the upper edge with a small box (see the Reinforcing Pockets Half-Pint Tip).

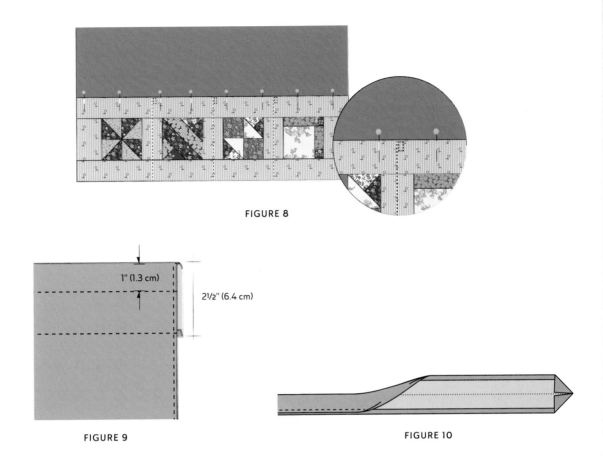

FIGURE 8

1" (1.3 cm)

2½" (6.4 cm)

FIGURE 9

FIGURE 10

11. Press under ¼" (6 mm) twice on the sides of the apron and topstitch close to the edge to secure.

FINISHING

12. Referring to **FIGURE 9**, fold the top of the apron under ¼" (6 mm), then fold it another 2½" (6.4 cm). Stitch close to the ¼" (6 mm) fold from the wrong side of the apron. Measure 1" (2.5 cm) from the top of the apron, then draw a line with removable marking pen across the apron width for the casing. Stitch on top of the line.

13. Fold under the long edges of the tie ¼" (6 mm), then press the tie in half. Press the ends in at an angle and edgestitch (**FIGURE 10**).

14. Using a large safety pin, thread the tie through the opening in the casing. Make sure the tie is centered, then sew a vertical line of straight stitching at the center of the apron to secure the tie and prevent it from slipping out in the laundry.

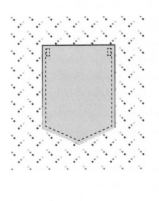

HALF-PINT TIP
Reinforcing Pockets

Any time you apply patch pockets or stitch dividers to create pockets, sew a tiny square or rectangle at the top of your topstitching for reinforcement.

Chapter 3

QUILT AND PROJECT TEMPLATES

Templates are printed reversed and without turn-under allowances for use with paper-back fusible web.

BEADS FOR CARRIE TEMPLATE

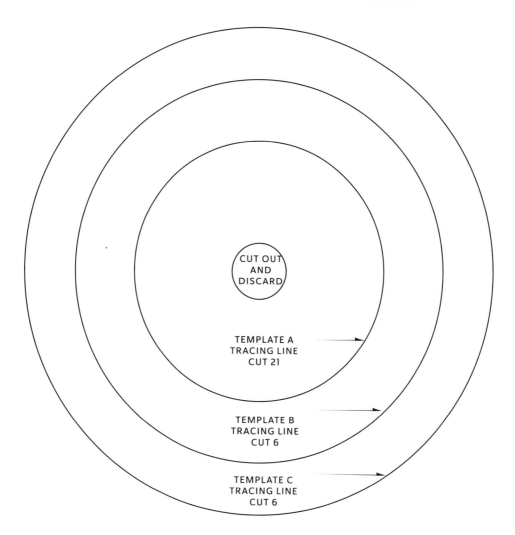

CUT OUT AND DISCARD

TEMPLATE A
TRACING LINE
CUT 21

TEMPLATE B
TRACING LINE
CUT 6

TEMPLATE C
TRACING LINE
CUT 6

BEADS FOR CARRIE
TRIMMING TEMPLATE

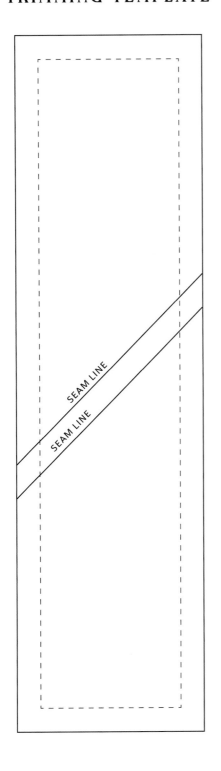

SEAM LINE

SEAM LINE

SINGING WILDFLOWERS
DIAMOND TEMPLATE

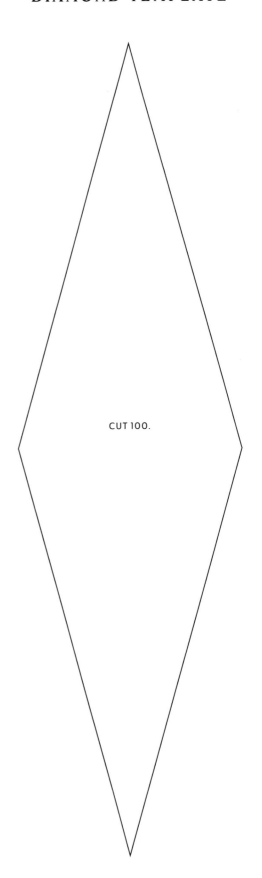

CUT 100.

A JOLLY DOLLY AFTERNOON

CUT 9 TOTAL OF EACH TEMPLATE
AND EACH TEMPLATE REVERSED.

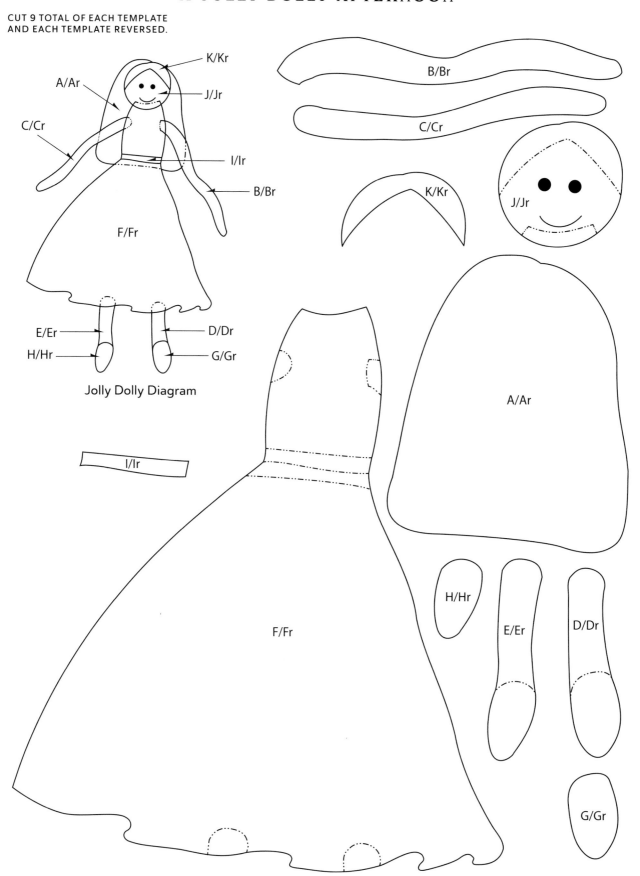

Jolly Dolly Diagram

PRAIRIE BLOOMS
TABLE RUNNER
FLOWER TEMPLATE

FLOWER TEMPLATE IS SHOWN AT 70%.
ENLARGE TO 140% TO USE.

When properly enlarged,
this square should measure
1" (2.5 cm).

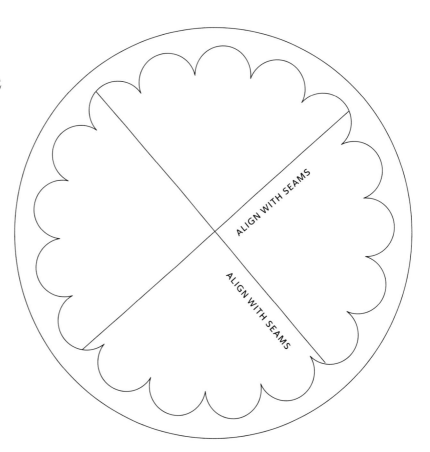

ALIGN WITH SEAMS

ALIGN WITH SEAMS

CROW PLACE MAT

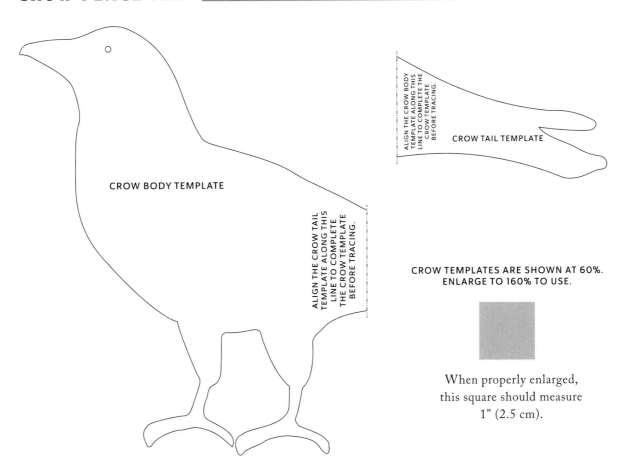

CROW BODY TEMPLATE

ALIGN THE CROW TAIL TEMPLATE ALONG THIS LINE TO COMPLETE THE CROW TEMPLATE BEFORE TRACING.

ALIGN THE CROW BODY TEMPLATE ALONG THIS LINE TO COMPLETE THE CROW TEMPLATE BEFORE TRACING.

CROW TAIL TEMPLATE

CROW TEMPLATES ARE SHOWN AT 60%.
ENLARGE TO 160% TO USE.

When properly enlarged,
this square should measure
1" (2.5 cm).

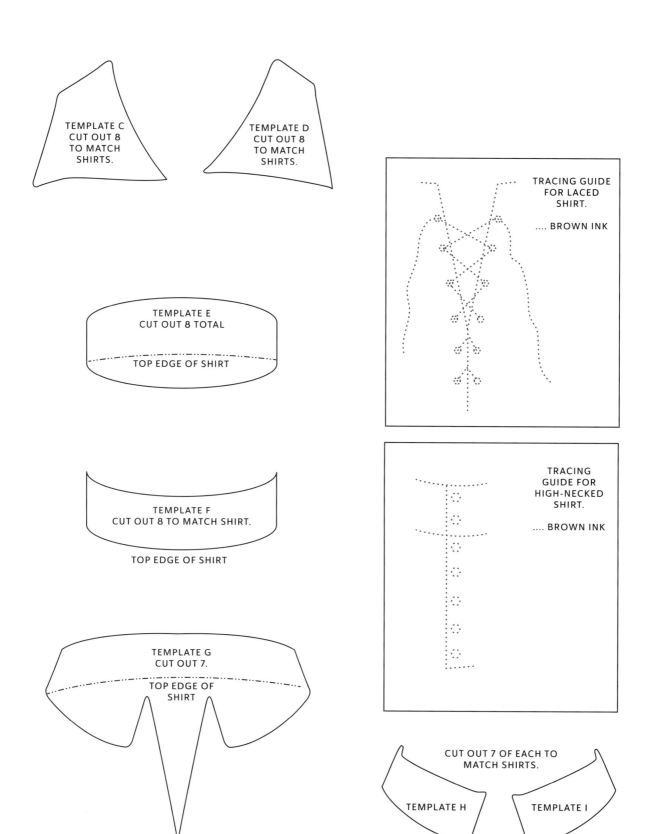

TEMPLATE C
CUT OUT 8
TO MATCH
SHIRTS.

TEMPLATE D
CUT OUT 8
TO MATCH
SHIRTS.

TEMPLATE E
CUT OUT 8 TOTAL

TOP EDGE OF SHIRT

TEMPLATE F
CUT OUT 8 TO MATCH SHIRT.

TOP EDGE OF SHIRT

TEMPLATE G
CUT OUT 7.

TOP EDGE OF
SHIRT

TRACING GUIDE
FOR LACED
SHIRT.

.... BROWN INK

TRACING
GUIDE FOR
HIGH-NECKED
SHIRT.

.... BROWN INK

CUT OUT 7 OF EACH TO
MATCH SHIRTS.

TEMPLATE H

TEMPLATE I

A SPRINGTIME OF SHIRTS

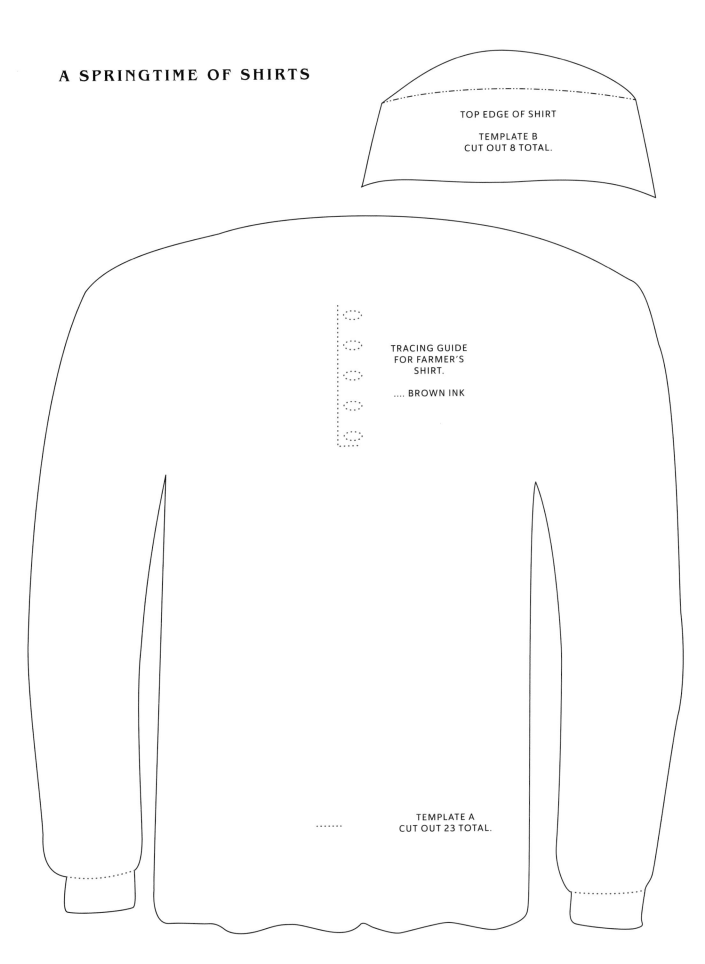

TOP EDGE OF SHIRT

TEMPLATE B
CUT OUT 8 TOTAL.

TRACING GUIDE
FOR FARMER'S
SHIRT.

.... BROWN INK

TEMPLATE A
CUT OUT 23 TOTAL.

BRAIDS, BONNETS, AND BOWS

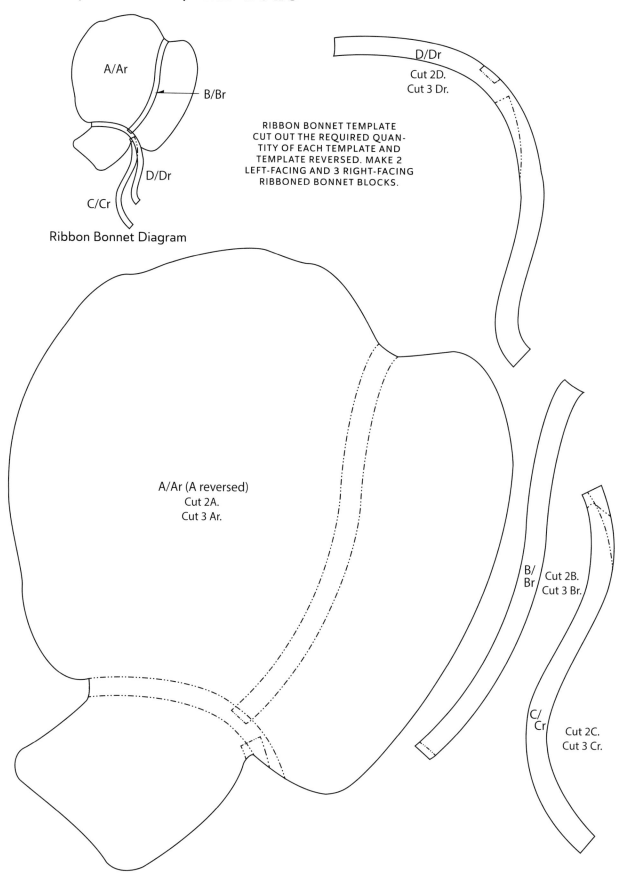

A/Ar

B/Br

D/Dr

C/Cr

Ribbon Bonnet Diagram

RIBBON BONNET TEMPLATE
CUT OUT THE REQUIRED QUAN-
TITY OF EACH TEMPLATE AND
TEMPLATE REVERSED. MAKE 2
LEFT-FACING AND 3 RIGHT-FACING
RIBBONED BONNET BLOCKS.

D/Dr
Cut 2D.
Cut 3 Dr.

A/Ar (A reversed)
Cut 2A.
Cut 3 Ar.

B/
Br
Cut 2B.
Cut 3 Br.

C/
Cr
Cut 2C.
Cut 3 Cr.

BRAIDS, BONNETS, AND BOWS

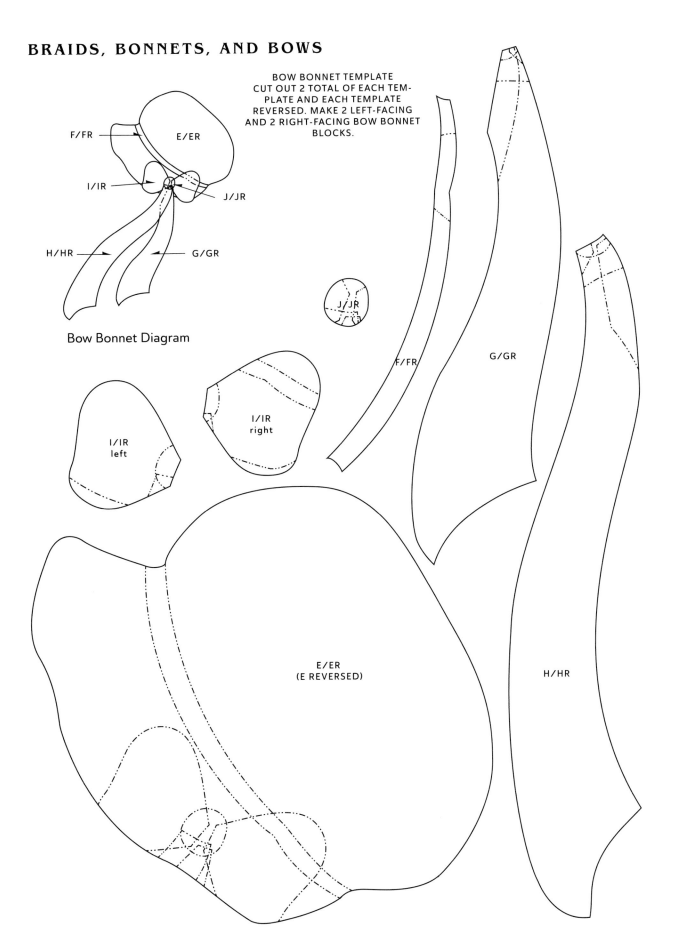

BOW BONNET TEMPLATE
CUT OUT 2 TOTAL OF EACH TEM-
PLATE AND EACH TEMPLATE
REVERSED. MAKE 2 LEFT-FACING
AND 2 RIGHT-FACING BOW BONNET
BLOCKS.

F/FR

E/ER

I/IR

J/JR

H/HR

G/GR

Bow Bonnet Diagram

J/JR

F/FR

G/GR

I/IR
left

I/IR
right

E/ER
(E REVERSED)

H/HR

BRAIDS, BONNETS, AND BOWS

RUFFLE BONNET TEMPLATE
CUT OUT 2 TOTAL OF EACH
TEMPLATE AND EACH REVERSED
TEMPLATE. MAKE 2 LEFT-FACING
AND 2 RIGHT-FACING RUFFLE
BONNET BLOCKS.

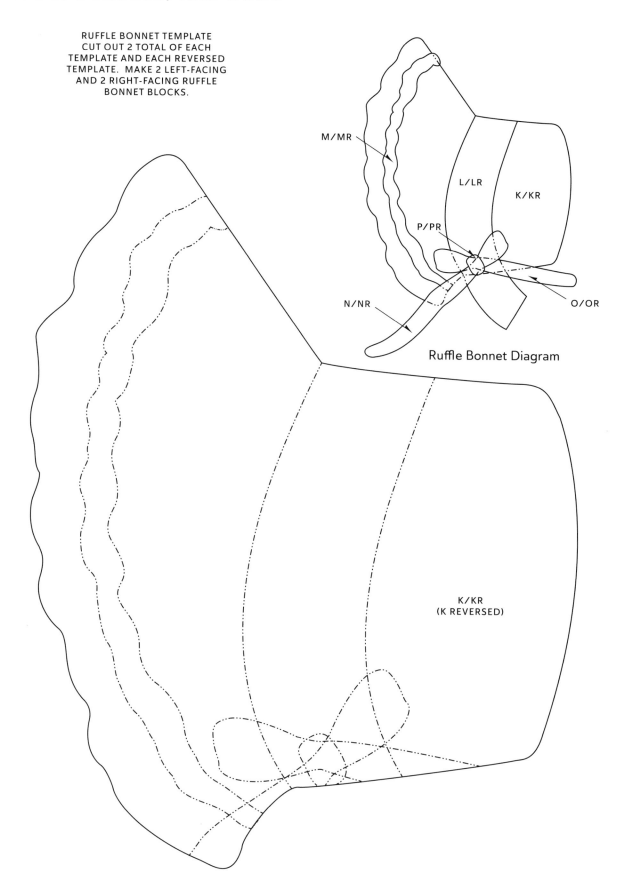

M/MR

L/LR

K/KR

P/PR

O/OR

N/NR

Ruffle Bonnet Diagram

K/KR
(K REVERSED)

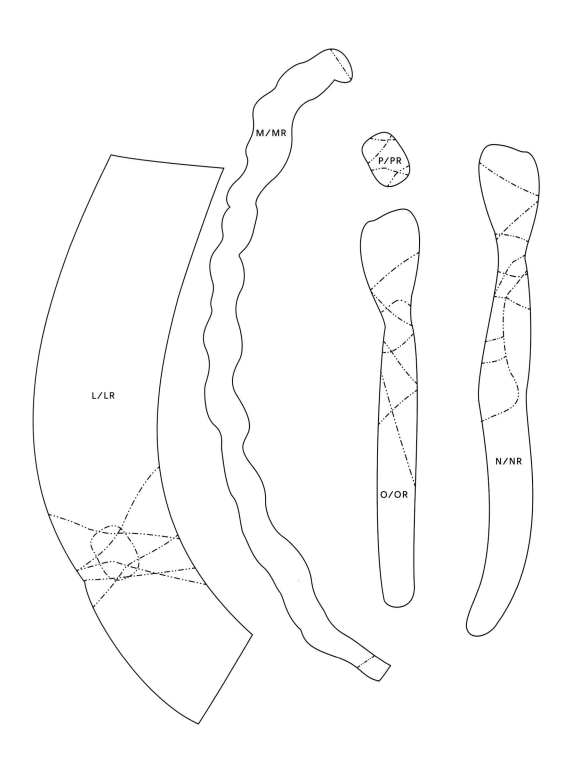

THREE SISTERS APRON

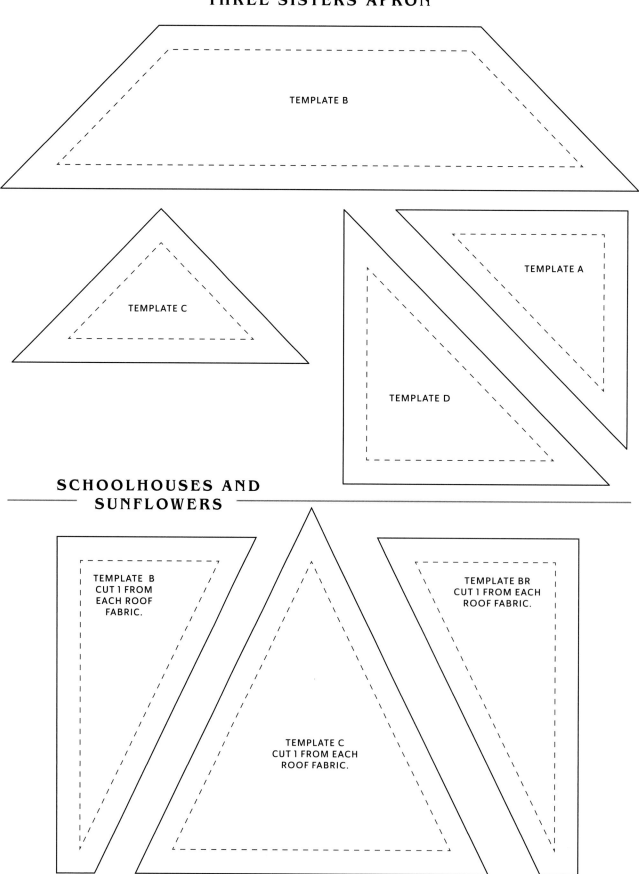

TEMPLATE B

TEMPLATE C

TEMPLATE A

TEMPLATE D

SCHOOLHOUSES AND SUNFLOWERS

TEMPLATE B
CUT 1 FROM
EACH ROOF
FABRIC.

TEMPLATE BR
CUT 1 FROM EACH
ROOF FABRIC.

TEMPLATE C
CUT 1 FROM EACH
ROOF FABRIC.

SCHOOLHOUSES AND SUNFLOWERS

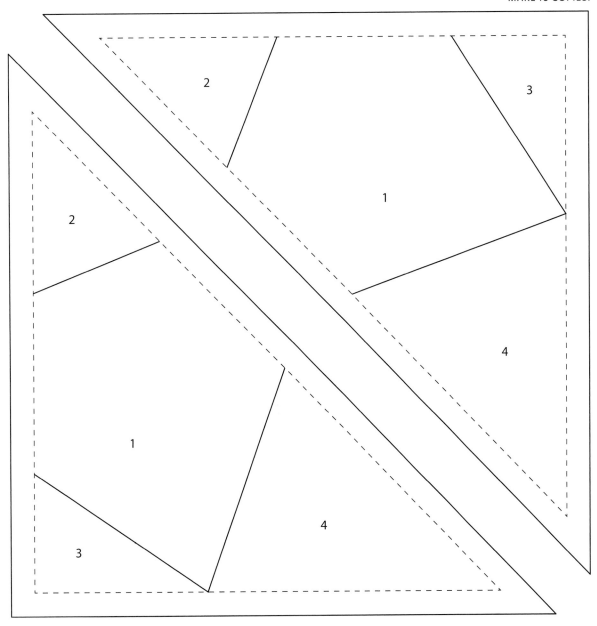

FOUNDATION MASTER G
MAKE 16 COPIES.

2

3

1

4

2

1

4

3

FOUNDATION MASTER F
MAKE 16 COPIES.

TEMPLATE A (BELL)
CUT 4 FROM GREY TEXTURE

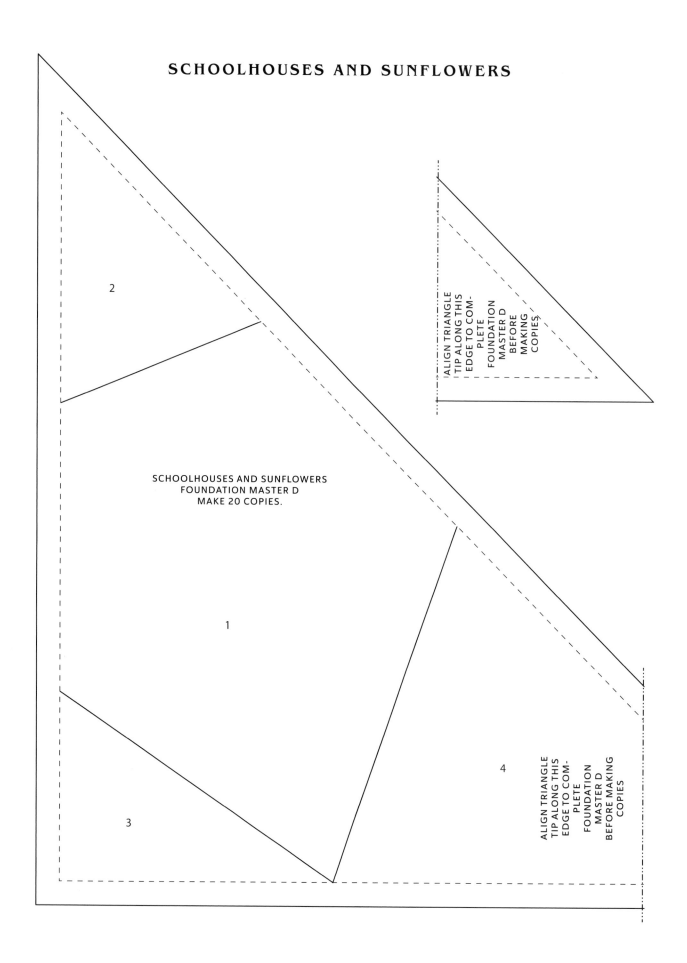

2

ALIGN TRIANGLE
TIP ALONG THIS
EDGE TO COM-
PLETE
FOUNDATION
MASTER D
BEFORE MAKING
COPIES

SCHOOLHOUSES AND SUNFLOWERS
FOUNDATION MASTER D
MAKE 20 COPIES.

1

4

ALIGN TRIANGLE
TIP ALONG THIS
EDGE TO COM-
PLETE
FOUNDATION
MASTER D
BEFORE MAKING
COPIES

3

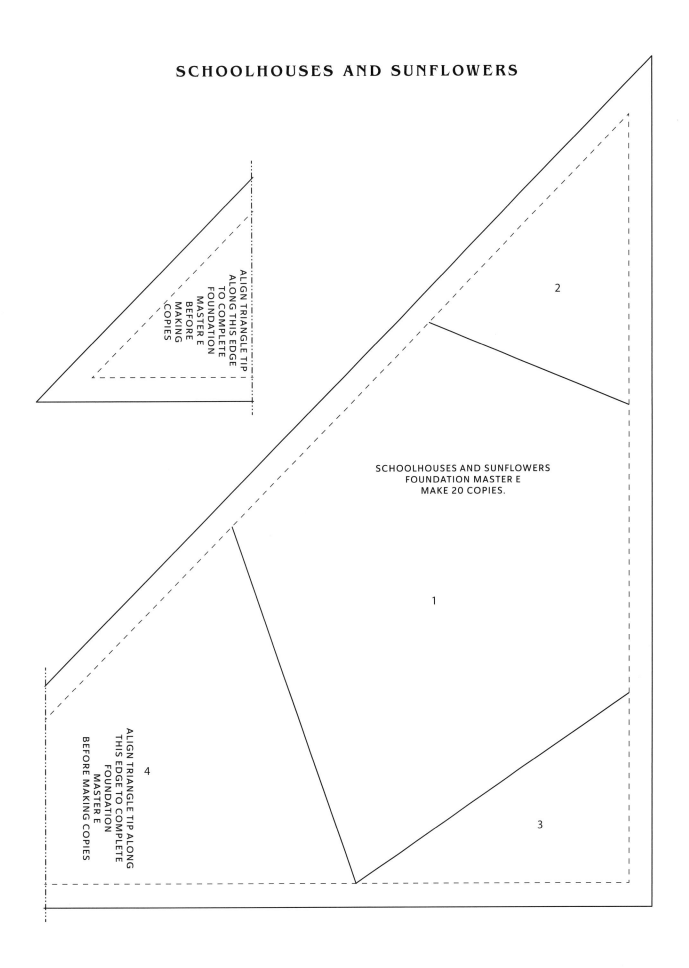

ALIGN TRIANGLE TIP ALONG THIS EDGE TO COMPLETE FOUNDATION MASTER E BEFORE MAKING COPIES

2

SCHOOLHOUSES AND SUNFLOWERS
FOUNDATION MASTER E
MAKE 20 COPIES.

1

ALIGN TRIANGLE TIP ALONG THIS EDGE TO COMPLETE FOUNDATION MASTER E BEFORE MAKING COPIES

4

3

ACKNOWLEDGMENTS

The works of Laura Ingalls Wilder were the inspiration for this book. Her unforgettable tales of pioneer life in nineteenth century America enchanted me when I was a child and still charm me today. The stories and images in her books provided endless inspiration for the quilts in this book. And the Andover Fabrics Little House collections gave my quilts just the right aesthetic.

Thank you to the wonderful friends who made quilts for this book. I can't tell you how lucky I feel to have friends like you all. The biggest of hugs to Laurie Bevan, Kathy Lewis, Sherri Driver, Kathryn Patterson, Katie Melich, Martha Haynes, Rae Strauss, and Gwen Barlow. I can never thank you enough, and will be your weeding slave for all time.

Longarm quilters are the angels that make quilts sing. Thanks to Karen Dovala of The Quilted Moose for her fine work and good taste. Special thanks to Donna Smith of Quilted for You Colorado. Donna broke speed records (without compromising the quality of her quilting) during a crazy month of finishing quilts for me. I'll weed your gardens, too.

Thanks and gratitude for your patience and hard work to Amelia Johanson and Jodi Butler, my wonderful editors. Thanks, too, to everyone at F+W Media who made this book possible. Your work brings so much happiness to so many people.

Drew, Bria, Nessa, Dani, Jake, and AJ, you're the loves of my heart and have all been so encouraging. I'd be lost without you. A special thank you goes to Bria for walking me through computer minefields and to Drew for being there when I needed a kind ear. And I can't leave out Daisy, my 160 pound, 4-footed exercise partner and stress reliever. Thanks for getting me out of my chair. Hugs to Moth, Buddy, and Bumble for joining me in the sewing room at all times of the day and night. Your fur is a permanent part of all my quilts.

Last, but not least, thanks to Dan for putting up with fabric hanging from the rafters, peanut butter and jelly sandwiches for dinner, and colored pencils underfoot. Loving and supportive, funny and distracting…you're the best!

DEDICATION

This book owes its existence to my mom, who shared her great love of fabric with me, and to my dad, who read me to sleep at night. Although they've both been gone for many years, their gifts have stayed with me and brought me much joy. Thanks, Mom and Dad!

METRIC CONVERSION CHART

TO CONVERT	TO	MULTIPLY BY
Inches	Centimeters	2.54
Centimeters	Inches	0.4
Feet	Centimeters	30.5
Centimeters	Feet	0.03
Yards	Meters	0.9
Meters	Yards	1.1

ABOUT LAURA INGALLS WILDER

In 1867, Laura Ingalls Wilder was born in a cabin on the edge of the unending forests of Wisconsin. Her family was a pioneering one, traveling by covered wagon through Kansas, Minnesota, and the Dakota Territory. As an adult, Laura wrote the story of her childhood (and her husband's) in the nine books listed. The books contain her memories of grasshopper plagues and dangerous rivers, laughter and music, and the joy of a job well done. In addition, her descriptions of the unspoiled lands of nineteenth century America stay with the reader forever. I know, because I can still see the grasses rippling in the wind from horizon to horizon and hear the birdsong of the wild prairie, even though I've never been there. These books are so special, so unusual, that they're simply not to be missed.

Little House in the Big Woods
Little House on the Prairie
Farmer Boy
On the Banks of Plum Creek (Newbery Honor Book)
By the Shores of Silver Lake (Newbery Honor Book)
The Long Winter (Newbery Honor Book)
Little Town on the Prairie (Newbery Honor Book)
These Happy Golden Years (Newbery Honor Book)
The First Four Years

ABOUT THE AUTHOR

Laura Stone Roberts is a former assistant editor of *McCall's Quilting* and *McCall's Quick Quilts* magazines and is skilled in all types of piecing and appliqué. She began quilting as a new mom thirty years ago and soon landed a job at a quilt shop where she discovered the joy of being with other quilters and sharing what she'd learned. Laura began teaching classes way back then, adding techniques as her skills grew. She has now been a quilting teacher for over twenty-five years. In 1997, she found herself in England without a guild, so she started one that grew to fifty-two members from seven countries. That guild was a great source of camaraderie and fun, and is still thriving today.

When it comes to fabric, Laura loves batiks and florals and clear bright colors. Her stash was epic. It had taken over a room and a half, and even though Laura gave fabric away to family and friends, the stash (and the mess) continued to grow. Luckily, before she was crushed under her piles of fabric, she found a way to calmly prune and organize the accumulated 'treasure' of two decades. Happily her project was a success, and her stash remains organized, accessible, and pettable today.

Laura still works as a contributing editor for *McCall's Quilting* in addition to being a freelance editor for book publishers and fabric companies. Her goal is to share her knowledge and love of quilting with others so they find as much joy in fabric and thread as she does.

Make classic quilts and patchwork with contemporary style!

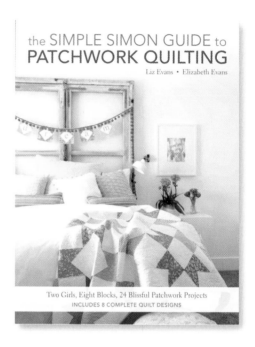

Mountain Mist Historical Quilts
Linda Pumphrey
ISBN 978-1-4402-4559-6
$24.99

The Simple Simon Guide to Patchwork Quilting
Elizabeth Evans and Liz Evans
ISBN 978-1-4402-4544-2
$24.99

This beautifully curated collection showcases 14 designs from the celebrated Mountain Mist Series. The unique marketing campaign, which offered a free quilt pattern with every Mountain Mist batting purchase, inspired generations of quilters throughout the twentieth century. In *Mountain Mist Historical Quilts*, author Linda Pumphrey recreates her favorite patterns—from art deco-inspired designs to intricate appliqués and traditional blocks—with current fabrics and techniques. The result: timeless designs that are as stunning today as when they were first introduced in the 1930s and 1940s.

In this sophisticated guide to quilting and sewing, popular Simple Simon and Company bloggers—and sisters-in-law—Liz Evans and Elizabeth Evans show you how to create traditional quilt blocks with a modern feel. Written with beginners in mind, *The Simple Simon Guide to Patchwork Quilting* invites you to get creative with step-by-step directions for making colorful quilts, stunning skirts and accessories, and unique home decor. Whether you're new to quilting or simply looking for inspiration, you'll love this stylish approach to traditional patchwork.

QuiltingDaily

For nearly a decade, Quilting Daily has been the place to learn, be inspired, and enjoy other quilters just like you. We bring you expert advice from our magazine editors, book editors, and Cate Prato, the editor of Quilting Daily.

ERRATA CAN BE FOUND AT
WWW.QUILTINGDAILY.COM/ERRATA